ARNHEM

ARNHEM
NINE DAYS OF BATTLE

CHRIS BROWN

YUMA COUNTY
LIBRARY DISTRICT
2951 S. 21st Dr. Yuma, AZ 8536
(928) 782-1871
www.yumalibrary.org

All images are copyright of the author or publisher, unless otherwise stated.

First published 2014
by Spellmount, an imprint of The History Press
The Mill, Brimscombe Port
Stroud, Gloucestershire, GL5 2QG
www.thehistorypress.co.uk

British Library Cataloguing in Publication Data.
A catalogue record for this book is available from the British Library.

isbn 978 0 7509 5380 1
Typesetting and origination by The History Press
Printed in Great Britain

CONTENTS

ACKNOWLEDGEMENTS

As ever, I am indebted first and foremost to my wife Pat, who has been a tower of strength in encouraging me to take on each of the writing projects that have been part and parcel of my life for more than a decade. I would have struggled without the access that I have had to four websites: www.arnhem1944fellowship.org, www.defendingarnhem.com, www.paradata.org.uk and, most of all, www.pegasusarchive.org. Between them, these sites provide the student of the battle in and around Arnhem and Oosterbeek with a wealth of information. I am particularly indebted to Mark Hickman of the Pegasus Archive for putting the diaries of the different units of the 1st Airborne Division into the public domain, and to Niall Cherry of the Arnhem Fellowship for the effort he puts into organising the regular fellowship newsletter and the various battlefield walks and lectures that help to maintain interest in this remarkable feat of arms. I am obliged to the Dreyeroord Hotel in Oosterbeek – a significant location during the battle, when it was widely referred to as the 'White House' – for its hospitality, and I should also like to thank Philip Reinders for his exceptional generosity in driving me around the battlefield and for taking the time to give the manuscript a 'once over' when it was still at a rough and ready stage. Fiona McDonald of the public library service in Lerwick, Shetland, has been assiduous in locating several volumes that are very difficult to obtain – I cannot thank her and the rest of the staff there enough.

INTRODUCTION

There are battles and there are iconic battles. Arnhem is most certainly one of the latter. It is hard to say what makes a battle iconic – there are no universal factors. The battle may be a victory for the smaller army, or it may herald a reversal of fortune in a long or especially arduous struggle. When we take an interest in a specific action it may be out of admiration for – or distaste for – a leader or army or it may be a product of our interest in the history of a nation, region, religion or ideal. It may be no more than the fact that we like the uniforms, literature or romance of a certain place or time.

Personally, I could point to a number of convergent streams. In all probability the very first 'grown-up' book I ever read – at the age of 9, I think – was Major General Urquhart's account of his experiences in Arnhem and Oosterbeek in September 1944. Shortly after that, and probably as a consequence, the first novel I read was *The Cauldron*, which I still think is one of the finest war novels ever written. It has occurred to me more than once that it would make great television – the only medium that would allow enough time for the development of the characters and a full portrayal of the story. It is, to say the least, unusual for a historian to give credence to a novel, but *The Cauldron* was written (under the pseudonym 'Zeno') by a man who served in the Independent Company in North Africa and Arnhem. Known at the time as Kenneth Allerton (and before that as Gerald Lamarque), the author described the battle from the point of view of an infantry soldier, which provides a unique perspective. It is even more unusual for historians to cite authors who produced their work while serving a life sentence for murder in Wormwood Scrubs prison – where he also wrote several successful novels and screenplays – but such is life.

Those two books were certainly instrumental in my interest, and none of the many hundreds of battle accounts from the Middle Ages to the Gulf Wars has made the same impact. Sometimes we cleave to a topic because of factors that are not entirely rational, though I do not subscribe to the idea that an irrational like or dislike is any less valid than a rational one.

In my case, there is also the matter of a dog – though not a dog that failed to bark. When I was a small boy, my family owned (or was owned by) a rather portly black Labrador bitch. My parents had not chosen to have a dog; my father's boss had asked him to look after

The cauldron.

his dog for a matter of a few days or perhaps a week. The nature of service life – my father was an officer attached to the Parachute Regiment at the time – is such that people sometimes move on to other pastures rather suddenly, and that was the last the family saw of the dog's owner for many years. The dog was called Judy and the owner was Jimmy Morrison, who had served as chaplain to 7th Battalion, King's Own Scottish Borderers at Arnhem.

Anyone with an interest in the Arnhem battle has the benefit of a massive amount of material. There are hundreds of Arnhem books and there are a great many personal accounts – more, perhaps, than for any other divisional battle. In a perfect world, with an unlimited amount of space and readers who were happy to read a 5,000 page book, one could produce a marvellous volume, which not only contained all of the material but collated it in some magical way that allowed every word and deed to be compared and then related to date and location. Since that is clearly not possible – the book would be the size of a piano – the writer must be selective, and inevitably subjective. The incidents related here were not chosen because they are particularly famous or even very significant; that was not the objective of the exercise. They were chosen for no better reason than it seems to this writer that they give a certain feel or flavour of the battle. There are a number of places where the recollections of one individual are in conflict with those of another. Some discrepancies are apparent rather than real. Unit diaries and personal accounts would seem to list a great many more than the twenty-two German armoured and armed vehicles that can be confirmed as being lost in action against the 1st Airborne Division. There is not necessarily any conflict at all. Unit diaries refer to vehicles that were put out of action but not necessarily destroyed. Since the Germans retained the battlefield, it should hardly be surprising that they were able to recover and repair a substantial proportion of the half-tracks, armoured cars, self-propelled guns and tanks that had been immobilised or put beyond immediate repair during the fighting.

As a rule I have chosen to form no opinion on inconsistencies of time or date that might arise from eyewitness material or from unit diaries. The men concerned wrote about what they had seen and how they had seen it. Some personal recollections also conflict with unit diaries, and a number of those diaries are in conflict with one another – and one contradicts itself. Again, I have largely avoided that as an issue. Several unit diaries had to be compiled from memory after the battle was over, and the others were kept up to date by exhausted and hungry men; men who were immersed in an arduous fight for their survival, and therefore had rather more pressing responsibilities than discharging a relatively insignificant administrative duty.

There are several excellent blow-by-blow chronological accounts of the battle, and I did not see any pressing need to write another one. This book describes the battle as I have come to see it and nothing more. Next month or next year some new selection of material may come to light that would radically change my appreciation of the rationale behind the planning decisions or the factors that led to defeat. It is extremely doubtful, though, that anything would reduce my admiration for the men who served at Arnhem and who were, in the words of Obergruppenführer Wilhelm Bittrich, 'incredible in defence'.

TIMELINE

1940

10–11 May: German glidertroops seize the Belgian fort of Eben-Emael in the first airborne operation in Western Europe. Their success inspires Churchill to order the formation of an airborne force to total 5,000 men.

22 June: No.2 Commando is assigned to a parachute and glider role.

22 November: No.2 Commando is renamed 11th Special Air Service Battalion and becomes the foundation of British airborne forces.

1941

10 February: The first British airborne venture, 'Operation Colossus' is mounted to seize and destroy an aqueduct in Calibri in Southern Italy. The operation fails to achieve its objective.

27–28 February: 'Operation Biting' is mounted to capture German radar equipment at Bruneval and is a success.

September: Formation of 1st Polish Parachute Brigade at Leven, Scotland under Major-General Sosabowski. The Poles invented and developed many techniques and practices which had a profound effect on the development of Allied airborne forces. The Brigade was initially raised for operations in Poland in support of the Polish Government in exile.

10 October: 1st Airlanding Brigade formed under Brigadier Hopkinson.

November: Brigadier Frederick 'Boy' Browning promoted to Major-General and appointed to command 1st Airborne Division.

1942

November: 1st Parachute Brigade and other elements of 1st Airborne Division are deployed to North Africa. Units are in action between 12–29 November at Bone, Beja, Souk-el-Abra and Pont-du-Fahs.

1943

July: Elements of the airborne forces are deployed in 'Operation Husky', the invasion of Sicily. Toward the end of the year 1st Airborne units are withdrawn to Britain to train for the invasion of Northern Europe.

1944

January: Major-General Urquhart takes command of 1st Airborne Division.

4 April: Montgomery is given control of 1st Allied Airborne Army and starts to formulate a plan to renew the offensive in Northern Europe.

June: A plan to land 1st Airborne near Caen as part of the Normandy campaign is abandoned due to the risk of high losses. Over the next two months at least a dozen proposed operations were abandoned either because they were unfeasible or because the advance to the

Seine was so rapid that the planned objectives were overrun before the operation could be mounted.

19–25 August: The battle and liberation of Paris.

1 September: Eisenhower assumes command of all Allied forces in Europe, superseding Montgomery.

2 September: Allied troops enter Belgium.

3 September: 2nd Army liberates Brussels.

7 September: 11th Armoured Division crosses the Albert Canal.

10 September: Eisenhower accepts Montgomery's ambitious plan for a massive airborne operation to seize the road from Neerpelt to Arnhem – 'Operation Market Garden'.

11 September: 15th Scottish Division crosses into the Netherlands.

16 September: Airstrikes in support of Market Garden begin throughout the Arnhem–Nijmegen–Eindhoven–Grave areas.

17 September: First lift of the British Airborne Division lands at Arnhem as the American 101st and 82nd Airborne Divisions land around Nijmegen and Eindhoven.

18 September: The second lifts of the three airborne divisions arrive.

19 September: Poor weather conditions in Britain prevent the deployment of the infantry battalions of 1st Polish Parachute Brigade.

20 September: Nijmegen Bridge is captured by the American 504th Parachute Infantry Regiment.

21 September: The infantry battalions of 1st Polish Parachute Brigade are dropped around Driel on the south side of the Lower Rhine. Arnhem Bridge is recovered by the Germans.

24 September: Lieutenant-General Horrocks' XXX Corps reaches lower Rhine.

25 September: Horrocks and Browning agree that Market Garden should be abandoned and 1st Airborne is withdrawn from Oosterbeek through the night.

1

PLANNING FOR DISASTER

By the late summer of 1944, two massive Allied forces had advanced across France from Normandy and were poised to break through into Germany. One of these bodies, known as 21st Army Group, consisted primarily of British and Canadian troops under the command of Lieutenant General Bernard Montgomery; the other – 12th Army Group – consisted of US forces led by General Omar Bradley. During the initial period of the invasion, Montgomery had had overall responsibility for tactical decisions, a position he retained until there were enough US formations in France to justify – in fact, demand – splitting the command structure by forming 12th Army Group. The first stage of the invasion had involved a long, hard fight for little territorial gain. Eventually, the German defence cracked under the strain, and both Allied army groups were able to make incredibly rapid progress for several weeks and the 21st Army Group reached the western borders of the Netherlands. The speed of the advance had been greater than expected, and the strain on the supply chain was enormous. By the end of August, the armies were tired, the logistical system was massively overburdened and the Germans had started to make what would turn out to be an impressive recovery.

Inevitably, the rate of the Allied advance slowed as resistance stiffened, and it became increasingly clear that a major initiative would be required. Montgomery – anxious to restore the situation and, if possible, bring the war to an end before the onset of winter – formulated a daring and innovative plan to deploy a massive force of airborne units to seize river crossings throughout the Netherlands and race a strong force of armoured and infantry divisions all the way to Germany. The plan adopted was named Market Garden. It would lead to the final German battlefield victory in the west and leave Montgomery with a long, narrow salient that cost a great deal but was of little value. The war would, after all, continue into 1945.

Although it is abundantly obvious that the men who conceived, planned and executed the Market Garden operation did not anticipate a defeat – no commander sets out to be beaten, after all – it is equally clear that, from the outset, the entire exercise had serious flaws. Some of these were recognised at the time and some were not. But even those that were, or should have been, anticipated were ignored or, even worse, actively suppressed.

The initial premise was not without merit. Had the operation been completely successful, the Allies would have secured the highway into the Reich that Montgomery and others truly believed would bring victory much closer. The advantages were potentially far-reaching. The war would have been shortened by a considerable margin, resulting in much less loss of life, money and other resources. The idea that there would have been an immediate collapse of the German Army, and consequently the Nazi state, does not really bear examination, but that was not the essence of Montgomery's analysis. It might not have been utterly inconceivable, but it was certainly less than likely.

Breaking into Germany's core industrial powerhouse in the Ruhr region would, however, have had major consequences. Allied commanders had had this in mind for some time. On 22 August Montgomery's chief of staff, Major General Francis (Freddie) de Guingand, had met with General Eisenhower to discuss and deliver Montgomery's current thinking, including a series of notes on general policy that the Field Marshal had written.

In Montgomery's view – as recorded in his memoirs – the route to victory was for '… the great mass of the Allied armies to advance northwards, clear the coast as far as Antwerp, establish a powerful air force in Belgium and advance into the Ruhr' (Field Marshal Montgomery, 1958). Disrupting and, in due course, destroying the German war industry would inflict a crucial, even deadly blow on the remaining power of the Third Reich, although Germany would not be utterly bereft of stockpiles of arms, ammunition and fuel. Even complete success in the Ruhr would not necessarily have brought the war to quite as sudden an end as all that; it would not, for example, have closed down production in that other industrial powerhouse, the Saar region.

Even so, given a successful Allied offensive into the Ruhr, Germany might well have been obliged to give up territory in the east more quickly, in order to shorten her eastern front and lines of communication – even at the cost of re-aligning right on, or even within, the border – although the Russians might not necessarily have been able to take full advantage of such a development. Although it is widely accepted that Stalin used the strain on his enormously long logistics chain as an excuse for not proceeding against the Germans in Poland at the time of the Polish Home Army's rising in Warsaw, his failure to press the battle did have some basis in reality. The Russian industrial and logistical effort was under huge strain and probably not capable of sustaining a deep, high-speed advance on a front broad enough to keep the Germans fully occupied and prevent them from making the sort of extensive reorganisation needed to keep the Russians out of Germany.

The expertise and will to carry out a far-reaching reconstruction certainly existed – as the German high command demonstrated in the western theatre in September 1944. Allied intelligence had identified that a great many German units were without effective command and control after the retreat through France, and also that there were a large number of headquarters, support and administrative units whose formations had effectively ceased to exist. However, it does not seem to have occurred to anyone that the German staff structure might be capable of combining these elements at such a remarkable rate and so effectively that they could form a defensive line offering serious resistance to the Allied forces. It is hard to imagine that in the event of a rapid withdrawal in the east the German command would have proved incapable of achieving a similar degree of reorganisation. In the west, the Germans had been retreating at great speed due to massive Allied pressure on the ground. They had suffered enormous casualties and losses in materiel and were at a much greater disadvantage in the air. A planned withdrawal in the east – though losses had been heavy there, too – might well have proved to be even more effective.

By the beginning of September, it was becoming evident that the momentum of the Allied advance across France could not be maintained without a major new initiative; the questions were the 'where' and the 'how'. In Montgomery's mind the answer was clear: a single, concentrated, full-blooded thrust into Germany. This was at odds with Eisenhower's general policy of fighting on a broad front, which would force the Germans to spread their forces thinly from north to south – a policy that conformed to the old military dictum that to defend everything is to defend nothing. There was some virtue in this view. If the German Army were kept fully occupied all along their western front, they would have little or no opportunity to gather the size of force needed to mount the sort of counter-offensive that Hitler – and, even at this stage, some of his generals – believed could turn the course of the campaign and force the Allies back across the Channel.

The drawback of the broad-front policy was that the Allied supply effort was already creaking under the strain of keeping a vast force in action over a front hundreds of miles long and also hundreds of miles from its only source of materiel. Equally, there were many problems that could arise from mounting what even Montgomery described as a 'pencil-like' thrust deep into enemy-held territory, not least the enormous commitment of men, armour, artillery and air support to protect the flanks of the narrow salient from counter-attacks.

Montgomery was, however, confident that a concentrated attack would bear the most fruit. Although the destruction of Germany's industrial base would certainly have had a major effect on the progress of the war on both fronts, it is still open to question whether a successful operation would have allowed the fast breakthrough that Montgomery envisaged. The Allied supply chain was already strained to the utmost, and there was no prospect of any significant improvement in the logistical situation until, as Montgomery recognised, the port of Antwerp could be secured and brought into action. This was not simply a matter of capturing the city. The Germans were still firmly embedded on either side of the roads to the port, and clearing those areas was likely to involve a good deal of hard fighting over a protracted period. Even if the Germans decided to abandon the city and withdraw from the water roads, it would not take much effort for them to damage the harbour installations at least enough to keep the port from being fully operational for many months.

Montgomery had been convinced of the value of a thrust into the Ruhr for some time. He was not persuaded by Eisenhower's opinion that the Allied armies should close up to the river Rhine and cross in great strength but on a broad front so that, while 21st Army Group overran the Ruhr, the US forces could conquer the Saar region and thus completely unhinge the German munitions industries. Montgomery believed – or perhaps chose to believe – that he had secured agreement in principle to his general plans from Eisenhower's other lieutenant in the ground battle, General Bradley. Either he was mistaken in his interpretation of Bradley's words or the

Standard paratroop supply container.

US general had had a change of heart, because when Montgomery flew to Bradley's Headquarters at Laval on 23 August it transpired that Bradley now believed the main thrust of his own army group should be a drive on Metz and thence to the Saar. Montgomery went on to meet with Eisenhower to press his case. According to Montgomery, Eisenhower accepted that 21st Army Group was not strong enough or adequately supplied to start a massive new offensive without US support or priority of resupply and that any such offensive must be made under the direction of a single officer – Montgomery.

Montgomery's initial request was that he should take over direct command of no less than twelve US divisions from 12th Army Group. That was too much for Eisenhower to accept, although Montgomery did secure an undertaking that the northern elements of 12th Army Group would be 'adequately supported' in terms of supply to afford the protection that 21st Army Group would need on its right wing when the new offensive got under way.

Whatever Eisenhower had meant and whatever Montgomery had interpreted that to mean, it soon became apparent that the left wing of the US army was not getting the logistical support it needed – a fact reported to Montgomery by his liaison officer at Bradley's Headquarters. Montgomery decided to press his case and sent a message to Eisenhower on 4 September. Effective communications were not the easiest thing to achieve, since Eisenhower's own headquarters were at Granville in Brittany and almost unbelievably had no direct telephone or radio link with the headquarters of either Montgomery or Bradley. Montgomery's message reiterated his earlier suggestions and comments – chiefly that in his opinion the Allies had reached a stage in the campaign where a thrust to Berlin was likely to be successful, that the supply situation could not provide adequate support for two major offensives and that a thrust into the Ruhr was much more likely to bring about a successful march on Berlin than an operation with the same target but emanating from the Saar.

The message was sent on 5 September. Eisenhower's response did not arrive until 7 September, and then it contained only the second half of the message – the first part would not arrive for another 48 hours. The first part of the response, however, made Eisenhower's decision absolutely clear. He had come to the conclusion that 'No reallocation of our present resources would be adequate to sustain a thrust to Berlin' and that his policy was to occupy both the Saar and the Ruhr. He considered that once this had been achieved, the ports of Le Havre and Antwerp would be in Allied hands and it would be possible to support either or both offensives. But he went on to say that he had '… always given and will continue to give priority to the Ruhr, RPT [repeat] Ruhr, and the northern advance' (Field Marshal Montgomery, 1958).

Montgomery's response was to give a brief outline of his current supply and transport difficulties, but repeating the view that a '… reallocation of our present resources of every description would be adequate to get one thrust to Berlin' (Field Marshal Montgomery, 1958). Clearly Montgomery was still not amenable to Eisenhower's broad-front policy, and he soon had another issue to factor into his thinking. On 9 September, he was informed that a new German weapon – the V2 rocket – had made its first strike on London. Such intelligence as there was seemed to indicate that the rockets would be coming in some number, launched from sites in the Netherlands. Montgomery had already identified a route through the city of Arnhem as being the most promising avenue for a new offensive, and the V2 situation reinforced his view. Accordingly, he met with Eisenhower again on 10 September, this time at Brussels, where a knee injury prevented Eisenhower from leaving his aircraft. Yet another attempt to persuade Eisenhower to give 21st Army Group first call on any and all resources to facilitate an advance to the Ruhr and then Berlin failed to move the US general from his policy. But in the light of increasing German strength to his front and the new V2 attacks, Montgomery did secure backing for 21st Army Group to move on Arnhem. He was left in no doubt that he would not have all the logistical support (or control over a very large portion of 12th Army Group) that he wanted – a fact Montgomery recognised in a signal to Eisenhower on 11 September. He was, though, now in a position to press on and had already been given control over an additional force – 1st Allied Airborne Corps – which he intended to use in his new offensive. It was not the meeting with Eisenhower on 10 September that prompted Montgomery's decision, but rather a meeting the same morning with General Dempsey, commander of 2nd Army, and General Browning, the Airborne Corps commander. The basic premise for Operation Market Garden had already been formulated before Montgomery even went to Brussels; he was just looking for more support to carry it out.

The operation envisaged was well within the norms of airborne warfare. Parachute and glider troops would land behind enemy lines, secure a number of objectives – in this instance the river crossings

over the Meuse (or Maas), the Waal and the Neder Rijn – and then
hold them until relieved by ground troops. This was no different in
principle to operations that had taken place in North Africa, Sicily
and Normandy, but the scale was immense and the distance that the
ground troops would need to cover was considerable – the 'airborne
carpet' over which British XXX Corps would advance was to stretch
for about 60 miles. In theory, XXX Corps would start its advance
from the Meuse–Escaut canal, through the area of Valkenswaard
and join up with the US 101st Airborne Division under General
Maxwell Taylor.

The 101st's area of operation would consist of more than
25 miles, from Eindhoven to a point just short of Grave. This was an
enormous undertaking for a single division, but of the three airborne
formations the 101st would also have the shortest period of contact
with the enemy. It was also expected that the Germans would have
to concentrate their efforts on delaying XXX Corps and therefore
have little to commit to the battle against the 101st.

German troops and armour at Arnhem.

The US 82nd Airborne Division, under General James Gavin (at 37, the youngest US officer to take command of a division since the Civil War in the 1860s), would have responsibility for taking the bridges and securing the path northwards from there to the far side of Nijmegen – a distance of approximately 20 miles. As well as seizing bridges, the 82nd would also have to secure the Groesbeek Heights to the east of Nijmegen, to protect the flank of XXX Corps' advance from German attacks coming out of the Reichswald Forest.

At the same time, the British 1st Airborne Division, supported by the 1st Polish Independent Parachute Brigade, would seize the Arnhem road and rail bridges and form a bridgehead on the far side of the Neder Rijn that would include the whole city of Arnhem. All the airborne formations would, naturally, be lightly equipped, with little artillery support and limited supplies, but they would not have to hold out for very long. According to the plan, the leading formation of 2nd Army – General Brian Horrocks' XXX Corps – would have advanced to Arnhem in 24 hours, or 48 hours at worst, with XII Corps and VIII Corps to the left and right of the axis of attack, which would – it was assumed – put more pressure on the German defence by drawing forces away from the main battle.

Montgomery's concept of a massive force advancing across the Rhine, through the Netherlands and into Germany was bold and impressive, but not necessarily viable. Amassing the size of force that he had in mind – at one point he was thinking of an army of forty divisions – would have involved bringing US formations under his control, which would probably have been difficult to reconcile with political and public opinion in the United States. But even if that were possible, the operation could only be mounted at the expense of the supplies needed to sustain the advances of General Patton and the operations of General Devers to the south, though in fact relatively little of Devers' supplies came through Normandy. This too would be a public relations problem. Were it possible to find the forty or so

Polish paratroops.

Polish paratroops waiting to embark.

divisions that Montgomery wanted for the drive to Berlin, would it have been practical to maintain them in the field? The unexpectedly rapid advance across France and into Belgium had already proved to be too much of a burden for the available logistical effort – indeed one British division had been left behind on the Seine for lack of petrol and other supplies, and their transport had been removed to bolster the supply chain.

There might well have been political resistance from the French, too. The French government in exile and its military leaders had limited influence, but they still probably had rather more than was justified by their contribution to the general war effort since 1940. By September 1944, the French army was well into a phase of reconstruction and was a significant force once more. French support, at a time when co-operation was so crucial, might have been hard to retain in a situation where the war was to be carried deep into Germany before the liberation of France was complete.

There was also the matter of the condition of the army. The leading formations of the British, Canadian and US forces had been in more-or-less continual action for three months. The men were tired and their equipment was worn. Undertaking a massive offensive might have provided a fillip to their morale in the short term, but strong German resistance – and there is no reason to believe that the troops would have faced anything less – might have proved too much for divisions that had already fought so hard for so long. The same factor applied to the Russians. Soviet divisions had fought at least as hard, and for rather longer, as the British, Canadian and US forces, so there was no guarantee that they would be able to continue to exert the same pressure on the Germans as they had in the past, even if their logistical and industrial effort was up to the task – a highly questionable assumption, bearing in mind that their logistical chain was even longer than that in the west.

On the other hand, the offensive had certainly run out of steam, the Germans were clearly requiring discipline and confidence, and

Collecting supply panniers.

Supply containers on the Wolfheze–Arnhem railway line.

Supply pannier from Drop Zone 'V'. (Courtesy of Philip Reinders)

autumn was approaching. Shorter days, colder weather, more rain and fog would all militate against fast movement and would also be likely to put even more strain on the logistical effort. It would become harder to move material up to the front and there would be increased demand for various items – particularly bulky materiels like food, fuel and winter clothing.

The approach of winter would bring another practical problem: the western Allies had never really fought a winter war. Britain and France had been at war with Germany through the winter of 1939–40, but there had been virtually no fighting at all. The Germans on the other hand had done two hard years of winter campaigning in the infinitely more challenging environment of Russia. The lessons learned, particularly in 1941–42, had been costly ones, but the Germans knew what they were doing when it came to fighting in the cold.

The risks posed by Market Garden were considerable, but the potential benefits were huge. There was a real possibility – and not just in the opinion of Montgomery and his staff – that the war could be brought to a successful conclusion before the end of the year. It might not mean that the troops could be home by Christmas, but at least the fighting would be over.

If the operation were successful, the Allies would have the opportunity to do more than neutralise the German industrial complexes in the Ruhr and thereby seriously undermine Germany's ability to continue the fight. They would be able to secure the basis for a huge advance across open country to Berlin, though the supply issue would still hamper that. Whether such an advance could be mounted and maintained all the way across Germany would still be open to question, but the blow to German morale would potentially be a very serious matter for their hierarchy. That said, if the Allies proved unable to make rapid headway eastward, there might not be Montgomery's hoped-for quick conclusion to the war.

The loss of the Netherlands might not be such a great issue to the German public, but fighting on home soil would be a different matter. Hitler, Goebbels and Himmler had made repeated assertions about the impregnable nature of the home defences, but these must have seemed rather hollow by the late summer of 1944. It was possible that the will of the nation might crumble in the face of a new offensive, and Hitler's regime could collapse. On the other hand, the fact that the war had been carried on to German soil might achieve little more than a stiffening of the resolve of the people and the army. There is a widespread belief that the Germans would have been prepared to give up the fight in the west in order to concentrate on the eastern front and that the British, US and Canadian forces – 'and increasingly the French' – would have had a relatively easy path to Berlin. There are weaknesses, though, in that assumption.

So long as Hitler could rely on the obedience of various internal security and political forces of the Reich – and, of course, the Waffen SS on the battlefield – there was a good chance that the army and the people could be kept in line. It is all too easy to assume that Germans would be more inclined to surrender to the western Allies than to the Russians, but there was no guarantee that they would surrender at all. German officers may have thought wistfully of the possibility that there could be an armistice in the west while the war continued in the east, but in reality the political hierarchy of the Reich would not countenance surrender – they were surely aware that there could be no agreement with the western Allies that would allow the continuation of the Nazi state in any form or that they, as individuals, could remain in government. Since they were all destined for the death penalty in the event of defeat and capture, they really had no option but to fight on to the very last gasp. Moreover, there was no prospect of securing any kind of agreement with the western Allies that did not include the Soviet Union. Churchill and Roosevelt may not have had any illusions about the nature of Joseph Stalin, but they were committed to the defeat of Germany. Nothing else would be politically possible. After years of sacrifice, the only settlement that

would have been acceptable to public opinion in Britain, the United States or Russia was the complete and unconditional surrender of Germany.

The operation Montgomery envisaged would effectively demand that the US forces operating to his south had to halt to conserve fuel. This would be difficult for US political and military figures – and hard for the general public to understand since both Devers and Patton were making good progress. Patton was certainly unimpressed, though he was not actively opposed to a major thrust in principle and rather admired the concept of the plan. Naturally Patton would prefer his own force to be given the task of breaking through the German defence and therefore have priority for fuel – he was quoted by Chester Wilmot as saying 'my men can eat their belts, but my tanks have got to have gas' (Chester Wilmot, 1952).

Despite the political difficulties, Eisenhower accepted Montgomery's view that a plan to make a dash across the Netherlands was viable and agreed that extra resources would have to be diverted to 21st Army Group. He drew the line at making the operation the sole priority for supply, instead telling Montgomery that it would be a priority, not *the* priority. Montgomery, however, chose to interpret Eisenhower's support as a promise to ensure that 2nd Army, the leading formation in 21st Army Group, would have first call on whatever material was available.

Eisenhower and Montgomery had clashed over the general policy of the Allied offensive and about the need to provide the Market Garden operation with everything it might require, leading to the incident at a meeting in which Eisenhower was obliged to remind Montgomery that he was not the supreme commander and famously told him – 'Steady Monty, you can't speak to me like that. I'm your boss' (Chester Wilmot, 1952). Montgomery backed down. It was, after all, reasonable that an American should have overall control of policy given that the US was providing the bulk of the combat troops, aircraft and logistical support in terms of both materiel and transport – quite an undertaking given the scale of the war in the Pacific.

Patton's superior, General Bradley, had also expressed major concerns about the operation, but was willing to support it, though not at the cost of bringing Patton to a complete halt. He told Patton that he could undertake minor operations – really armoured reconnaissance on a grand scale – but not that he could force a major battle or commit himself to an extensive advance. There simply was not enough fuel to sustain more than one major offensive.

Patton's own fuel situation was not quite as critical as either Bradley or Eisenhower had been led to believe. Third Army really needed the better part of 400,000 gallons every day to keep its advance moving and that was much more than Patton could hope to receive. His troops, however, had liberated an enormous stockpile of petrol and diesel from the Germans, which had not been reported to Eisenhower's staff at Supreme Headquarters, Allied Expeditionary Force (SHAEF). His supply officers had also developed a practice of collecting material from other Allied formations whenever the opportunity presented itself. Moreover, Patton had concluded, quite correctly, that if he advanced his troops into situations where they would have to engage in major battles, his superiors would not be able to deny him the resources to carry on the fight. To some degree this was a matter of common sense. If Patton's army continued to make progress, it would be unwise to prevent him exploiting his situation. Anything else would merely give the Germans a chance to reorganise and therefore present a more effective defence. Additionally, there was a matter of perception. It was believed that the US public might not be especially happy about their sons and husbands coming under Montgomery's command. He had something of a reputation for being a little cavalier with the lives of troops that did not hail from the British Isles – and, arguably, from England in particular. The prospect of an all-US army being stopped in its tracks to allow Montgomery a free hand might prove to be very unpopular.

The Market Garden operation did have a genuine military rationale – the potential gains were believed to be worth the risks, and in principle it was not a rash stab in the dark. Even so, personal factors were significant. Some of the decisions made by both Montgomery and Browning were strategically and tactically questionable and their motivation was not always as professional as it might have been. For both men, their personal ambition caused real problems for the operation. Montgomery was determined that there should be a single crushing attack and that he, if at all possible, should be the man at the helm. If he could not be supreme commander in Europe, he certainly wanted to be leading the most important part of the campaign. If he could get his army into Germany and threaten Berlin, he would be in the driving seat, if not actually the captain of the ship.

Although the Market Garden operation was really not at all typical of Montgomery's approach to battle, the plan seemed to present an opportunity for 21st Army Group to be the leading element in the war in the west. Even if it failed to bring about a major German collapse – and it is important to remember that it might have done – it would still put the British Army, and therefore Montgomery, in the spotlight. However important the operations of Patton or Devers might be from a wider military perspective, the perception of the whole world would be that British and Commonwealth troops were the ones who were leading the fight. If Montgomery's forces raced across Germany and captured Berlin, history would see him as the man who won the war – Patton saw the situation in much the same light and was equally determined that he, not Montgomery, was the man for the job. A good deal has been made about the personal and professional rivalry that existed between these two generals, and it cannot be simply dismissed – they had already demonstrated a marked degree of competitiveness in the Mediterranean – but it is easy to exaggerate the importance of that competition. They were both ambitious career soldiers engaged in the greatest conflict the world had ever seen and that rivalry would have existed between any two generals.

The road to Berlin and his place in history were undoubtedly factors in Montgomery's mind when the operation was conceived, and it encouraged him to accept opinions from his subordinates which, in any other circumstances, he might not have taken at face value. His reputation for careful planning and caution was much deserved and had served him and the Allied cause very well in the past. It would be an exaggeration to say that Montgomery now cast his habitual conservatism aside and plunged headlong into the project without consideration – his determined stance over supply priority shows that he did not take the risks lightly – but he was, perhaps, rather less critical in his analysis than usual and overly reliant on the advice of some of his subordinates. He was also overly confident about the capabilities of others – and, indeed, of his army – particularly the ability of General Horrocks' XXX Corps to perform the remarkable feat of making an advance of more than 60 miles in 24 hours, or 48 hours at most.

As commander of the 1st Allied Airborne Corps, General Browning's contribution was crucial in forming Montgomery's opinion on the feasibility of the operation. Well connected and described, most appropriately, by several writers as an accomplished 'Whitehall warrior', Browning was eager to get his troops into the battle.

Browning had served in the First World War with some distinction, but he had had absolutely no senior command experience in battle. He had been involved in the development of British airborne forces almost since their inception and had created an aura of expertise that did not persuade everyone but made a serious impression on many of his colleagues and superiors. His practical experience away from the battlefield was more limited than many realised. He had made only two parachute jumps, was injured on both occasions and so was not a properly qualified parachute soldier. Being a qualified glider pilot helped Browning's reputation, though in fact all of his flying experience had been gained in the Airspeed Hotspur, a much smaller and lighter aircraft than the Horsa, Waco and Hamilcar gliders that would carry men to battle in September 1944.

Browning did have a very real talent when it came to furthering the interests of the airborne forces with the political and military hierarchy, but he had become obsessed with the desire to have a major tactical role in a battle – any battle. The Airborne Corps had only recently come under Montgomery's command and was the only major force that could be considered a strategic reserve, so it was natural that Montgomery should have given thought to how that force might be committed to an operation that could breathe new life into the campaign and also consulted Browning about the capabilities of the corps. He advised Montgomery that the operation as planned was viable and that the three airborne divisions and the 1st Polish Independent Parachute Brigade were equal to the task. There is considerable doubt over whether Browning actually used

Horsa glider.

the famous phrase that he thought 'we might be going a bridge too far' in discussions with Montgomery prior to the operation, though after the battle he clearly told Major General Urquhart that he had done so. If he really had used the phrase it would have indicated that he had not fully grasped the point of the exercise. If the airborne forces did not secure all of the crossings to enable the ground forces to create their corridor across the Netherlands, the whole operation would have been a failure; it would not actually matter which of the crossings was not secured because failure to hold any one of them would compromise the entire plan. This was not lost on the planners, and a huge stock of bridging material and thousands of engineers were assigned to the operation to ensure that one or more bridges could be erected with great speed, although that would depend on getting a vast convoy of vehicles to where they were needed along a single road that was already full to the brim with combat troops and supply columns.

If there is some doubt over Browning's 'bridge too far' comment before the plan was put into effect, there is even more doubt over Montgomery's assertion after the battle that the operation had been 75 per cent successful. In fact, since the 'airborne carpet' over which XXX Corps was to advance was never completed, the operation was a total failure.

Browning's anxiety to get his force – and himself – into battle was understandable in the sense that he was the commander of an elite formation built to fight, not to wait in camps for a call that never came. There would have been something badly wrong if he had not wanted to get his troops into action. Equally, if he had any doubts at all about the ability of his troops to achieve the objectives he would have made them clear to Montgomery. It is, of course, quite possible that he had complete confidence in his subordinates and believed that all of the formations in his command were ready for battle, but he must have been aware of the shortcomings in brigade- and divisional-level training in the British 1st Airborne Division, and, if he was not, he certainly should have been. As corps commander, it was part of his job to ensure that everything that could be done to make his formations battle-ready had been done and, if it had not, to put officers in place who would ensure that it was. Browning's assurance that his men had been properly prepared for the fight was a crucial factor in the decision to press ahead with Operation Market Garden – any doubt he might have expressed about the readiness of his command would have been an admission that he had failed in his professional duties.

For the best of reasons, Browning was very unhappy with the airlift arrangements. Naturally he would have preferred the entire force to be airlifted in and brought into action in one massive operation, but clearly there was not an adequate supply of aircraft to do that, and even if there had been, the traffic management challenges over the landing zones would have been enormous and possibly insurmountable. Since a single lift was clearly out of the question, he would have preferred to have two lifts staged on the first day of the battle to ensure that each of the divisions would derive as much benefit from the element of surprise as possible, and in particular to allow the entirety of British 1st Airborne Division to be committed to the fight at the earliest opportunity as they had the most challenging task. This would have had a more profound effect than simply putting more men on the ground – important though that was. Spreading the lifts over three days meant that Urquhart was obliged to commit a large portion of his division – in fact, the three strongest combat units in his force – to the defence of the dropping and landing zones that would be required for the drops on days D+1 and D+2 (18 and 19 September). If the division had been flown in on day one, he would effectively have had three times as many infantrymen to commit to the battle – probably enough to overcome the German defenders who successfully blocked the routes of two out of three of the battalions of 1st Parachute Brigade as they made their way from the landing zones, through

Oosterbeek and on into Arnhem itself. Additionally, the very fact that the British were protecting open spaces told the Germans exactly where the second lift would arrive and allowed them to concentrate and commit forces accordingly. Browning did make strong representations about the distance between the landing zones and the target as well as the prolonged airlift plan, but was unable to persuade the air commander of the importance of surprise or of the fact that an airborne division – like any other formation – was designed to operate as a single entity, not in disparate sub-groups.

There were a number of practical barriers to achieving Browning's preference. Staging two lifts in one day would have required at least a significant portion of the aircraft to leave the ground before dawn on 17 September. Not all of the British aircrew had had sufficient training in night flying to make this a viable proposition, and the

Arnhem landing zone.

majority of the US aircrew were in the same situation. The night-flying issue was not simply a matter of getting the aircraft off the ground and into their correct formations in the dark and early dawn; if there were to be a second lift, a large proportion, if not all, of the aircraft would be returning from their second sortie after dusk so there was a risk of collisions and lost aircraft. Neither the United States Army Air Force (USAAF) – providing the vast majority of the planes – nor the Royal Air Force (RAF) could afford to lose any of the precious transport aircraft, so the reluctance of the air planners is understandable. Once the Market Garden operation had been concluded, the air forces would still have to find the men and machines to discharge the wider obligations of the transport command units.

The issue of the standard of night-flying training is not entirely convincing. The US 82nd and 101st Airborne and the British 6th Airborne had been dropped into Normandy by night in June, so it is hard to see why that could not have been accomplished in September, except for one significant factor that no commander could influence – no moonlight. The element of surprise would, all things being equal, have been enhanced by landing the formations at night rather than in the middle of the day, but as the flyers would have been unable to identify the landing zones it simply was not practical.

There was also the matter of refuelling and maintaining the aircraft between the first and second sorties. Although Browning was confident that this could be achieved, there was real doubt about the viability of such an undertaking. The staffs of every airfield in Britain were already under immense strain and could not, realistically, be expected to redouble their efforts.

When it came to pressing the issue of the remoteness of the landing areas, Browning had another problem. The planning staffs of the chief air force commander – General Lewis Brereton of the USAAF – and of transport commands had constructed a schedule for the delivery of the airborne troops in a short space of time.

They had had a good deal of practice due to the number of proposed operations that had not gone ahead, and Brereton was adamant that there could be no modifications to the scheme.

This was to cause all sorts of problems large and small for each of the formations in 1st Allied Airborne Corps; but for the British 1st Airborne Division it would be disastrous. Browning was quite right to argue for more appropriate landing zones, but there was a limit to how far he could press his case. In the first week of September, he and Brereton had already fallen out over Operation Linnet II to the point where Browning had threatened to tender his resignation. In the British Army, this was the customary means of making a determined stand against the views of a superior – a step up from asking for your orders in writing if you believed that what was being asked was impossible, impractical or just terribly ill-advised. To Brereton it was the next best thing to wilful disobedience. Browning really could not take the same route again. If he had, his resignation would have been accepted, and the US general Matthew Ridgway would have replaced him. Ridgway certainly had more practical command experience than Browning and was a man of robust views, but whether he would have been able to persuade Brereton to alter the air plan in any regard, let alone to the extent of changing the British landing zones, is open to question. Brereton had made Ridgway aware of the situation with Browning and that he was in line for the job if Browning were to resign. He would hardly have done so if he had thought that he would face serious opposition from his own appointee.

Browning's attempt to sway Brereton came to nothing, and perhaps he should have been prepared to resign over the matter. He should certainly have taken it up with Montgomery who, if necessary, could have approached Eisenhower to exert pressure on Brereton, but he chose not to. The Airborne Corps had now been assigned to 21st Army Group and Browning became the chief – if not only – source of advice to Montgomery on airborne issues.

Browning's lack of practical experience now became a serious problem, but so did Montgomery's eagerness to force the pace of the campaign by bringing the Airborne Corps into the mix. In effect, each encouraged the other toward an undertaking that was to have grave consequences for thousands of men but could only be successful with the very best of good fortune in a number of areas. The weather had to remain fine, the ground forces had to make good time over difficult country, the airborne forces had to overcome the challenges of being too far from their targets and arriving on the field in dribs and drabs, and – most significantly – the Germans had to fail to take adequate steps to foil the operation.

It is all too easy to point to failures in analysis, planning and execution of any failed, or even successful, operation. History is about what did happen rather than what could have happened. Military planning, however, does involve detailed consideration of what may be achieved – it is never an exact science. Even if an operation goes according to plan, a multitude of unforeseen and unforeseeable consequences will generally emerge after the battle. Some of this is due to the fact that no intelligence picture is ever utterly complete, some to the certainty that no projection from analysis is ever perfect, some from what the Prussian general Carl von Clausewitz labelled 'friction', and some from sheer fortune – good, bad and even what, at the time, seems simply indifferent.

Major planning flaws are glaringly evident at every stage of the Market Garden operation. Some of the problems were avoidable and some not, but overall the perception that the planning staffs had become 'victory happy' is not unjustified. Of course, an ambitious operation carries risks, and everyone must have been aware of this. What is open to question is the extent to which the risks were adequately assessed.

The overall condition of the German forces in the west was certainly poor compared to what it had been in June. The losses of men and materiel – particularly armour and aircraft – were more than could be sustained by German society and industry, but the plight of the Nazis was not as dire as it seemed to the Allies. By the end of the second week of September, it should have been clear at all levels of the Allied command structure that resistance was stiffening and that the German military establishment would continue to reassert its high professional standards.

Additionally, it should have been obvious just from looking at maps of the terrain that as Allied forces moved eastward the countryside would become more advantageous to the defender than the attacker. The succession of major rivers running through the Netherlands provided more than barriers to the Allied advance. By posting military police at river crossings, the Germans were able to effectively stop retreating troops from making their way home and instead gather them into units that could be assigned to formations that in turn could be returned to the front to impede Allied progress. This was facilitated by the remarkable quality of training throughout the German armed forces. Merely gathering men together into ad hoc bodies did not turn them into first-class cohesive front-line units, but it did provide a basis for reorganisation to a much more effective degree than would have been the case for British or US troops in similar circumstances.

Experience should have told Allied planners that this was the case. Britain and Canada had been at war with Germany since 1939 and the US since 1941, so the German military was hardly an unknown quantity. To ignore the possibility that the Germans would be able to stage some level of recovery in retreat effectively spurned the lessons that should have been learnt in North Africa and in Italy.

Amid all the wider strategic and political issues, there was also the pressure to get 1st Allied Airborne Corps into battle. The advance of 2nd Army towards the Netherlands had ground to a slow pace if not an absolute halt. In part, this was a matter of the German Army recovering at an increasing pace from its retreat across France and, of course, the exhaustion of the leading elements of the Allied force, particularly General Horrocks' XXX Corps. It was also a matter of supply –

Obsolete French Renault tank used by the Germans for training.

the transport lines for food, replacements, ammunition and petrol had been stretched much further and far more quickly than anyone had believed would be either necessary or possible. Additionally, so long as German garrisons continued to occupy the Channel ports, there was little prospect of the situation improving to any marked degree until the area surrounding the Scheldt estuary could be cleared of German forces to secure the approaches to Antwerp for Allied shipping and bring the harbour facilities into operation.

There was no guarantee that simply assigning more units to the forward edge of the battle area would have any noticeable impact on the situation, even if those units could be kept properly supplied. In any case, there was no reserve pool of units on the continent waiting to be committed. The sole strategic reserve on the western front was the Airborne Corps. Of the five airborne (and one 'air-portable') divisions available, one – the British 6th Airborne – had only recently returned from the battle in Normandy and had not yet completed the demanding and time-consuming business of rebuilding its units and absorbing replacements for losses. Another division – the US XVII

Airborne Division – had been fully trained in the United States before being transported to Britain, but was not yet considered ready for battle. The air-portable division (52nd Scottish), which had originally been trained for alpine warfare, was ready for action, although not designed or trained to be dropped straight into battle but rather to be delivered to existing airstrips. The remaining formations consisted of British 1st Airborne Division, the US 82nd and 101st Airborne Divisions, and the 1st Polish Independent Parachute Brigade. These were all considered to be combat-ready, though in fact there were some serious deficiencies in the training of the British division that would show up all too clearly during the Market Garden operation. In total, the combat elements of these formations amounted to a strength of rather more than 35,000 men, and not just any men, but particularly fit and well-motivated soldiers who had consciously volunteered for more hazardous duty than most infantry soldiers.

Clearly this was a substantial force that could not simply be left on the shelf indefinitely. In fact, the total number of men redeployed from the main body of the armed forces to support the airborne initiative was more than the 35,000 soldiers. Each division had a 'tail' of transport and other staff which would follow them across the Channel once battle was joined and be on hand to give the combat troops the logistical – and other – support they would need, assuming that once the primary operation had been concluded each division would continue to fight as a 'normal' infantry formation. The 'tail' units would be vital as and when the divisions took up a conventional combat role, but the manpower this entailed was little more than the tip of an iceberg.

For obvious reasons, an airborne force is somewhat redundant unless the aircraft capacity exists to deliver the troops to wherever they need to be. In addition to the combat formations and the seaborne 'tail' elements, a vast quantity of aircrew, fitters, engineers and technical staff had to be kept in a state of readiness if it was ever going to be possible to mount a major airborne operation.

Even that was far from being the whole story. The troops and the aircrew required the services of thousands of ancillary staff, from cooks to tailors, not to mention a veritable host of civilians working on airbases or in factories to provide the meals and equipment – much of it either completely specialist or being manufactured as a special 'airborne' variant, necessary to ensure that the airborne formations would be ready for battle when the time came. By September 1944, there must have been many people who wondered if that time would ever actually come at all. Ever since the Normandy invasion, a succession of plans had been proposed and operations prepared, only to be cancelled or abandoned. Some were overtaken by events due to the exceptional speed of the advance of 21st and 12th Army Groups through France. One or two had been cancelled thanks to outbreaks of realism and common sense among the planners when it became apparent that this or that proposal was impractical.

A good deal has been written about the succession of abandoned operations, and there is some dispute about exactly how many there were. It seems most likely that there had been a total of fifteen, but several of these affected no one other than a very small number of staff officers since they never really progressed beyond being a concept for consideration. On balance, it should be assumed that the planning process did more good than harm. Every plan that got as far as a detailed consideration of objectives, aircraft requirements, loading tables and manpower estimates should have been subject to an assessment to see precisely what lessons could be learnt and applied to future projects. Some of the proposed operations were not entirely realistic. In one such plan, British 1st Airborne Division would have been dropped on a Normandy beach if an Overlord landing had failed. In such an event the naval forces would have had more than enough to do trying to extricate the formation that had been landed by sea without adding to the burden with a division landed from the air, including the strong possibility that many paratroopers could have ended up drowned in the Channel.

Another plan, 'Operation Raising Brittany', was supposed to land the division behind German lines, where it would form a secure base for French guerrilla bands and harass the infrastructure of the German Army. It does not seem to have occurred to anyone that, even if French fighters had swarmed to this airborne pocket in their thousands, an airborne division could hardly be expected to train them into useful combat troops in short order, or that the Germans would probably commit armoured units able to crush the division quickly. There has to be some question as to how seriously anyone took these plans. Maybe there was never any real intention to put some of them into effect, or perhaps they were really no more than a means of giving airborne planning staffs something to do.

The immediate predecessor to Operation Market Garden had been Operation Comet. It was essentially the same plan, with the same range of objectives, but achieved with only the resources of 1st Airborne Division. The operation would have started on 8 September, aiming for completion by 20 September with the arrival of the leading elements of XXX Corps at Arnhem to relieve the parachute troops and move towards Germany. It has been suggested that Comet might well have worked where Market Garden failed, and there is some justification for this view, though it does not really bear scrutiny. It is true that during the nine days between the planned launch of Comet and the commencement of Market Garden the German Army made tremendous progress in reorganising the shattered remains of their formations into viable combat assets, and that on 8 September the army was still in a state of confusion from its rapid retreat across France. It is even arguable that the arrival of the British airborne units at Arnhem, Nijmegen and Eindhoven might conceivably have brought about a state of panic and disorder that would have allowed XXX Corps to sweep aside any remaining resistance.

On the other hand, the units of XXX Corps were pretty much as exhausted as the Germans they had been pursuing for several weeks.

Nor is it clear that such fuel reserves as were available would have been enough to support a rapid advance by a large force over a distance of more than 60 miles, nor that, even given adequate reserves, there would be sufficient materiel to support the drive beyond Arnhem.

There is also the matter of the strength of the Airborne Division. Only one brigade could be assigned to the primary Arnhem objective, and although the bridge – or at least one end of it – was in fact held for longer than the Market Garden plan required and by a single battalion, there are a number of flaws in the assumption that this would have been the case under Operation Comet. For one thing, although the Arnhem bridge story understandably focuses on the exploits of 2nd Battalion, the Parachute Regiment, it is important to remember that it was not the only unit represented in the action. In total, Colonel Frost's force numbered more than 700 men, including gunners, engineers and a large portion of 1st Parachute Brigade Headquarters – though not the brigadier himself. Their stand was a remarkable feat of arms, but it should be remembered that although the German high command was aware of the significance of recovering the bridge, it did have rather more extensive battles on its hands around Oosterbeek and at Nijmegen. If, as Comet envisaged, the whole of 1st Parachute Brigade had managed to establish itself on both sides of the Neder Rijn on the first day of the operation, it would have been fighting in isolation. In essence, the brigade would have had to form two perimeters on the opposing banks of the Neder Rijn connected by the bridge itself, while facing all the enemy assets in the Arnhem area and without being able to call on the full strength of the divisional artillery regiment.

That is not the only consideration. Each of the other objectives would have had to be seized and defended by much smaller forces than was the case under the Market Garden plan. Since the chain of objectives was obvious from the moment the troops started

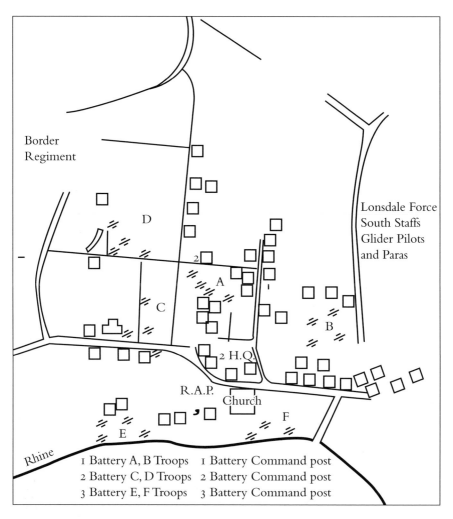

Border
Regiment

Lonsdale Force
South Staffs
Glider Pilots
and Paras

D

2

A

C

B

2 H.Q.

R.A.P.

Church

F

E

Rhine

1 Battery A, B Troops   1 Battery Command post
2 Battery C, D Troops   2 Battery Command post
3 Battery E, F Troops   3 Battery Command post

Gun positions around Oosterbeek Old Church

landing, the German command would have been aware – as it was
with Market Garden itself – that it needed only to secure one of the
river crossings between Eindhoven and Arnhem in order to totally
frustrate the entire operation. Although it is true that there would
have been fewer German units available to commit to actions along
the proposed corridor, the British force at each location would
have been so thinly spread that it is difficult to imagine that every
objective would even have been taken, let alone held until the arrival
of XXX Corps' tanks. Brigadier Hackett was confident that Comet

would be a disaster and was undoubtedly not the only person to be relieved when the operation was cancelled on 10 September just hours before it was to go ahead.

The planning of Comet and other cancelled projects proved to be of some value. In fact some of the documentation was merely over-printed with the title 'Market Garden'. Much has been made of the various staffs having only one week to prepare for the Market Garden operation, but all sorts of matters, such as loading schedules for aircraft and gliders, either were or should have been relatively straightforward. By this time army planners should have been totally familiar with how many troop transport aircraft were required for each paratroop battalion or how many gliders for an airlanding battalion, battery, squadron or troop. The various elements of the airborne forces may not have had the full-scale divisional exercises that would have been preferable, but they had loaded and unloaded their jeeps, trucks, carriers, guns and other equipment in and out of the gliders often enough to be able to do it quickly and effectively

Glider pilot's view.

on the eve of battle. It was, in fact, a vital aspect of their training. It was always on the cards that an airborne operation – especially one on a grand scale – might have to be put in place with great haste to take advantage of an unexpected opportunity.

This sense of readiness applied equally to the aviation aspects of the operation. Air force planners had spent a huge amount of time on questions such as how long it would take to get however many aircraft into the sky, to marshal them into the necessary formations and get the columns to a specified location, deliver their loads and return to their bases. The planners may have had only a week to organise the operation, but they were not starting with a blank sheet.

2

STRUCTURE OF BRITISH 1ST AIRBORNE DIVISION

The Parachute Regiment provided the majority of the infantry units within each of the two airborne divisions of the British Army in 1944. The term 'regiment' was – and continues to be – used rather differently in the British Army to most others. In the US or German Army, a regiment would generally have three battalions and operate as a single permanent institution. For the British, a regiment is a more nominal entity and often has a geographical dimension in the sense that all the battalions are recruited from a specific area. Any number of battalions might be raised under the same name, hence the men of the Airlanding Brigade were from 1st Battalion, the Border Regiment, 2nd Battalion South Staffordshires or 7th Battalion, King's Own Scottish Borderers. It was not unknown to have two battalions from the same regiment serving in one brigade, but it was not a general practice. Broadly speaking, the term 'brigade' in the British Army is rather close to the usage of 'regiment' elsewhere. Parachute brigades were something of an exception for the simple reason that if a parachute brigade was required for a task, clearly all of the men would have to be parachutists. The fact that 1st Parachute Brigade consisted of the 1st, 2nd and 3rd Battalions of the regiment is not exactly mere coincidence, but it was not, of itself, of any particular significance – 4th Parachute Brigade consisted of the 10th, 11th and 156th Battalions.

Raising a parachute regiment had been one of Churchill's many brainchildren, inspired no doubt by the success of the German operation to seize the fortress of Eben-Emael in Belgium in 1940 and perhaps by the much-quoted words of Benjamin Franklin to the effect that no prince, however wealthy and powerful, could protect his entire domain from a force of 10,000 men descending from the sky. Franklin had not, however, given any thought to the practical aspects of maintaining such a force once it was on the ground, though admittedly the business of keeping troops adequately supplied was rather more straightforward in the eighteenth century. He had also neglected to offer any wisdom on the topic of how the force might be extracted once its mission was accomplished or in the face of the kind of resistance that he rather assumed would not be forthcoming.

In popular perception, Market Garden is often, if not generally, seen as exclusively the province of the Parachute Regiment, though in reality gliders landed a large proportion of the division, including a considerable number of men who were actually members of the Parachute Regiment. The 1st Airborne Division consisted of nine infantry battalions (six parachute and three glider-borne) and, for the purposes of the Market Garden operation, the 1st Polish Independent Parachute Brigade, consisting of three further battalions. In total, the Airborne Division had a true 'bayonet strength' of around 6,000 infantry plus the men of the Glider Pilot Regiment who, unlike their counterparts in the US airborne formations, were trained to act as infantry soldiers once they were on the ground, though it was expected that they would generally take a less offensive role than the rifle battalions.

The remainder, like any other infantry division, was made up of artillerymen and the many arms of service that are required to keep the infantry battalions in action. Although all soldiers are expected to be capable of infantry combat, for airborne personnel that aspect of their training was, all in all, more developed than would have been the case in a conventional division. It was much more likely that airborne service corps, ordnance and supply staff, engineers and others would have to be more active in a combat role than their counterparts in other formations. This would stand the division in good stead in the nine days at Arnhem and Oosterbeek, all the more so since one of the infantry units – Colonel John Frost's 2nd Battalion – would be separated from the main body of the division before the end of the first day, and half of the other infantry units would be severely depleted in attempts to reach the objective.

The parachute and glider battalions differed in size and organisation. Each parachute battalion consisted of 613 men – 29 officers and 584 other ranks – and had only three rifle companies, instead of the four that was normal practice in conventional infantry units. Each company had 117 men (5 officers and 112 other ranks) and broadly followed the usual structure of four platoons, each consisting of three rifle sections, though the incidence of automatic weapons tended to be somewhat higher.

In addition to the rifle companies, there were various support elements that together constituted the headquarters company of 9 officers and 226 men, including an anti-tank platoon with Projector, Infantry, Anti-Tank (PIAT) weapons and two platoons of four 3-inch mortars whose vehicles and some of whose men were deployed to the battle area by glider. Battalion commanders seem to have had some discretion over their support assets and could opt to replace some of their mortars with Vickers gun teams. The Battalion Headquarters consisted of five officers and twenty-two men. The key word in all the strength of the battalion – and this applies to all the units in the division, not just the infantry elements – has to be 'theoretical'. For a variety of reasons, few units ever actually have their complete establishment available for duty at any given moment. Some men will be absent sick or injured, or for reasons unknown. On the eve of Market Garden, some men failed to return from leave on the assumption that whatever operation was being planned would – like so many others in recent weeks and months – come to nothing and that their absence for an extra day or two would not be of any significance. By some means, though, word does seem to have 'got around' and a number of men managed to make their way back to their units in the nick of time despite the challenges of travelling across wartime Britain with out-of-date leave warrants. It is remarkable that so few, if any, were picked up and detained by the Military Police. In addition to these elements, there are always a few men absent on courses or seconded for other duties. It is not always practical or possible to replace these men – some will only be absent for a matter of a few days – and in a specialist combat formation like the Airborne Division temporary replacement is well nigh impossible since it is not likely that there will be any significant number of trained parachute or glider soldiers to be found from other units or manpower pools.

Additionally, the very nature of an airborne operation means that there would almost inevitably be some men missing when the unit gathered at its forming-up area. It would only take one aircraft to fail to take off or be forced to abort for mechanical reasons, to get shot down or crash, and the men on board would be lost to their battalion for the foreseeable future. Also, there was always the possibility that men might be dropped prematurely (or late) or drift away from the landing zone on the breeze. Losing just one aircraft would mean that one platoon on the ground would be missing half of its personnel before the operation was fully under way. This would be a blow to the efficiency of any infantry unit, but more so to a battalion with only three rifle companies.

The decision to have three rifle companies instead of four was not irrational. It was never intended that parachute battalions should have to fight a battle to gain their objectives, but rather that they should be dropped very close to the target area – if not actually on top of it – and that they should, if necessary, fight to hold on to their ground. In that light, having only three companies meant that the battalion would be strong in defence and have most – though not all – of the assets of a conventional infantry battalion.

The major missing component other than the fourth company was the lack of the usual anti-tank platoon of 6-pounder guns. The thinking was that an anti-tank platoon would not always, or even generally, be a relevant asset to the battalion, and that it would make more sense to raise a number of specialist airborne anti-tank batteries that could be assigned to battalions as required. That decision certainly added a greater degree of flexibility to the airborne arm as a whole but had serious repercussions for Market Garden. The training structure failed to ensure that there was sufficient integration between the anti-tank batteries and the infantry battalions. Since they were not integral elements of each individual unit, there was not sufficient opportunity for one part to train alongside the other. Because of that, there was not as good an understanding of the principles of anti-tank combat as there might have been. In essence, the enemy armour has to be lured towards a place where the anti-tank guns will have a good field of fire from concealed and protected positions. It is simply not practical for an anti-tank gun to stalk a tank or for it to be unlimbered from its towing vehicle and deployed in an instant. Failure to take this on board led to reduced effectiveness and the loss of a number of guns and crews that could not be replaced. This was not the case, though, with the airlanding units. Each of the glider-borne battalions – 1st Border, 2nd South Staffordshires and 7th King's Own Scottish Borderers – had their own anti-tank platoons as a fully integrated part of the unit and were rather more effectively employed as a consequence.

The theoretical establishment of a glider-borne battalion listed a total strength of 864 men – 47 officers and 817 other ranks – and was therefore a little more than 25 per cent larger than a parachute battalion. In practice, the number of men and the selection of equipment varied from one operation to the next. Every battalion

South Staffordshires marching toward Arnhem.

in both 1st and 6th Airborne made changes to their organisation to take account of each of the operations to which they were assigned. Brigadier Hicks' 1st Airlanding Brigade – like the parachute battalions – had suffered heavy losses in Sicily, not least more than two hundred men who drowned when their gliders were released while they were still over the sea.

Each of the four rifle companies in the battalion consisted of six officers and 121 other ranks. The four platoons of the company retained the structure of three sections, but each had only seven men to give a platoon of twenty-four, including the platoon commander and his headquarters group. This allowed the entire platoon to be carried in a single Horsa glider, so that it would arrive on the battlefield as a single entity and, with any luck, in reasonably close proximity to the rest of the battalion.

Despite the slightly smaller size of an airlanding platoon, the overall combat strength of the battalion was larger than that of a parachute battalion. After the war, Brigadier Hackett would suggest that it might have been a better plan to assign the stronger airlanding

6-pounder anti-tank gun in action.

battalions to the seizing of the objective on 17 September and to commit the parachute battalions of 1st Brigade to hold the landing and drop zones. There are a number of strong points to his analysis. The most significant one, of course, is simply the greater strength of the units, though that would largely have been negated by the decision of General Browning to take his own headquarters – a superfluous addition in any meaningful sense – to the battlefield. Browning's Headquarters required a total of thirty-eight gliders, all of which were drawn from the allotted lift capacity of 1st Airborne Division and would otherwise have been available for the Airlanding Brigade on the first day of the operation. Instead, the South Staffordshires were forced to leave two rifle companies and various other elements behind, with the intention that they would rejoin the battalion as part of the second lift.

Brigadier Hackett's thinking was sound, but did not take account of the internal politics of the Airborne Division or the public relations aspect. The Parachute Regiment had already established a place in the hearts and minds of the British public as a romantic

Men of the South Staffordshires, after they were taken prisoner.

Troops of the Airlanding Brigade.

and exciting innovation in warfare and as an elite formation. But a number of the early projects undertaken had not been as successful as they might have been and the airborne element of the Normandy landing, though effective, had been overshadowed by the sheer magnitude of the rest of the operation. Operation Market Garden would put the Airborne Division firmly in the spotlight, and if anyone was going to accrue fame through a daring exploit it would most assuredly be the Parachute Regiment rather than the glider-borne battalions of the Airlanding Brigade.

A division – airborne or otherwise – must have any number of ancillary elements if the combat troops are to be adequately supported, and the Royal Engineers (RE) provided a considerable part of 1st Airborne. Each RE squadron was formed from a headquarters and three troops, each divided into two sub-units consisting of a lieutenant, a lance sergeant and 16–18 sappers (engineering troops). In total, a squadron should have had 150 men of all ranks, including no fewer than 17 officers. In common with virtually all units, the notional strength of the unit was seldom achieved. Captain Harry Faulkner-Brown, a sapper who served in 4th Parachute Squadron – the Royal Engineers element attached to 4th Brigade – made the observation that the squadron never had more than twelve officers at any one time.

Although the Airborne Division was classed as an elite formation, most of the constituent units had training and discipline issues. When Harry Faulkner-Brown joined his squadron at the start of 1944, several of the ORs (Other Ranks – all soldiers apart from the commissioned officers) had taken jobs in local businesses, a practice that was soon ended when a new commanding officer – the remarkably named Major Aeneas Perkins – was appointed and instilled a more rigorous approach. There were wider issues such as men going absent without leave or getting into trouble over drunkenness, fighting and general insubordination. To a degree this was a consequence of sheer boredom and frustration at being stuck in camp for long periods and the steady stream of operations planned, prepared for and then abandoned. The issue was recognised by General Urquhart and steps were taken – a number of officers were replaced and the situation improved, though not, perhaps, to the complete satisfaction of either the general or his subordinates.

One exception – though not, in fact, part of the Airborne Division – was the 1st Polish Independent Parachute Brigade, which General Sosabowski ruled with the proverbial rod of iron. The Polish contribution to the development of the British airborne force was considerable. Although the pre-war Polish army had never raised a parachute unit, parachuting was strongly encouraged as sport so there was a sizeable pool of officers and some other ranks with relevant experience. A large number of Polish troops made their way to Britain after the fall of Poland in 1938 and of France in 1940. In due course, 1st Polish Armoured Division was formed at Duns in Berwickshire and, at its peak strength, amounted to some 16,000 men. In September 1941, the 1st Polish Independent Parachute Brigade was formed at Upper Largo in Fife. Under General Sosabowski, the Independent Brigade developed new training methods and conducted experiments with equipment, including what British parachute trainers called 'the Polish Method' for directing a landing by spilling air from the canopy during the descent.

The growth of the parachute arm between 1940 and 1944 was mirrored by the progress of General Browning's career. In 1941, he was appointed to the post of commander of the newly formed 1st Airborne Division. He was assiduous in his advocacy of the new force, but not without causing a good deal of offence through his rather overbearing manner and his habit of behaving as though he had been appointed as the commander of all airborne forces. He travelled to North Africa and, not content with treating the US airborne officers as subordinates – including General Ridgway, the commander of US 82nd Airborne Division, who was his equal in rank – Browning committed an exceptionally bad breach of etiquette by making an unannounced inspection of a US unit, though he had absolutely no authority to do so. From this point on, Browning would put a good deal of effort into undermining Ridgway's reputation.

Browning had high hopes that the airborne forces would continue to be enlarged and that he would climb the promotion ladder.

General Sosabowski (left) and General Browning.

His concern was that Ridgway would be a competitor for the position of commanding general of all Allied airborne troops. Browning's ambitions were not limited to gaining control over US troops. Ever since the inception of the 1st Polish Independent Parachute Brigade he had campaigned vigorously, though unsuccessfully, to have that formation brought under the control of the British airborne establishment – headed, of course, by himself. His efforts were resisted by General Sosabowski and the Polish government in exile, both harbouring hopes – though not very realistic ones – that the brigade would, at some point, be deployed to Poland to help reinstate the government before the Russians could put their own people in place.

Browning's ambitions with regard to the Poles were not entirely unreasonable. The Polish Brigade notionally took their orders from their own government, but ultimately their quarters and equipment were provided – and their salaries paid – by the British treasury. All the same, Browning was perfectly well aware that the independence of the Polish Brigade had been agreed by both governments and that he was indulging in a spot of empire-building, which, with any luck, would further his own career.

Churchill's enthusiasm for the airborne warfare concept survived the general experience of airborne forces between 1941 and the summer of 1944. The Germans had staged a major airborne operation on Crete, which was successful in achieving its objectives, but the cost was high enough for Hitler to declare that 'the day of the parachute soldier is over'. British airborne operations in North Africa and Sicily had not exactly been unalloyed successes, but the British 6th and the US 82nd and 101st Airborne Divisions had been a vital part of the Normandy landings despite many aircraft failing to deliver the troops to their correct drop zones.

All in all, the parachute arm had received a good deal of favourable coverage in the press and from what today we would call army media relations – not to mention the considerable influence of General Browning. But the list of real successes was small. The Bruneval raid in 1942, led, coincidentally, by John Frost, had secured German radar equipment that helped to give the British an edge in the air campaign, but 1st Airborne Division had yet to be deployed as the single entity it was meant to form in battle and its track record was not especially impressive. The events of June 1944 went some way to changing the picture. On the eve of the Overlord landings, airborne troops of the US 82nd and 101st and the British 6th Airborne Divisions had been landed at critical locations across Normandy to secure bridges and neutralise German assets that could threaten the development of the beachhead. Despite a great many of the troops being dropped miles from the designated sites, the airborne aspect of the operation was an overall success and the reputation of airborne forces for determination and combat effectiveness received a well-deserved boost

The Normandy operations did not include 1st Airborne Division, though there were contingency plans for sending it to France if the landings did not go well. In fact, the division was not really combat-ready. It was still absorbing replacements for earlier losses and a fair number of men who had come to the conclusion that they might never go into action with the division and had requested – as was their right – to be returned to their original units.

Although elements of the division had fought with some distinction in North Africa, they had largely done so as conventional infantry units, and the airborne action in Italy had not been an unqualified success. The influence of the Parachute Regiment lobby was committed enough to ensuring that it should be entrusted with the portion of the operation that was most dramatic and newsworthy to have given little consideration, if any, to any proposition other than that 1st Parachute Brigade should lead the march into Arnhem and hold the objectives until relieved by XXX Corps. A major, and dramatic, achievement would help to keep the regiment in the public eye and perhaps ensure its continued existence after the war was over. Whether anyone actually articulated such a thought is open to question, but there was certainly some opposition to the Parachute Regiment as an institution. It was seen by many – and not without cause – as something of a private business. The airborne arm was not a popular concept in all quarters. General Browning had faced widespread opposition, even hostility, from various quarters at different times during the development period, but had managed to keep the airborne project intact in the face of the demand for manpower and despite the enormous costs involved – quite an achievement under the circumstances.

The RAF had, in general, seen the parachute and glider units as a cross it had to bear at the insistence of Churchill rather than a project with which it was fully engaged and to which it was genuinely committed. The price of its support had been that the first and final say on any decisions relating to the 'air' side of operations should lie with the RAF rather than with army planners. As a result, although the RAF would provide aircraft, it would drop the men or release the gliders to landing and drop zones that suited its own agenda and priorities and not necessarily the purpose of the mission. This was the primary problem with the Arnhem operation. In order to avoid what they perceived as an unacceptable risk to aircraft from the flak batteries at the bridge – though in fact the anti-aircraft gunners there had a reputation for being very poor at their jobs – the RAF planners chose the drop zones around Oosterbeek and Wolfheze, making the whole operation (to coin a phrase) not so much a matter of 'a bridge too far', but rather one of 'too far from the bridge'.

There was also considerable doubt in army circles about the value of forming a new regiment. A number of senior officers, and many who were career professionals rather than those for whom the army was a sort of paid pastime for the years before they retired to run the family estate, were of the opinion that any well-trained and properly led infantry battalion could be put to any task if given the relevant training and equipment. To these officers it seemed that forming an army within an army was of questionable value, and to make matters worse, since the new regiment was formed from volunteers from other units, it attracted the cream of the crop. To some degree at least they were quite correct. The Parachute Regiment arranged for recruiting parties to visit units all over Britain and North Africa, trawling for volunteers. It not only attracted men who were eager for action, but it could also send any that failed to make the grade in terms of fitness or intellect – or who were prone to rocking the boat or to ill-discipline – back to their units. The Parachute Regiment was therefore able to pick and choose its members at the expense of the army as a whole, and the infantry in particular. This was not the case for the airlanding units, which were formed from existing rifle battalions, though naturally there was a good deal of 'weeding out'. Men were also brought in from other formations, notably a considerable number of officers provided by the Canloan scheme, through which Canadian personnel were seconded to the British Army, a process that helped to offset the shortage of British officers and broadened the experience of the Canadian officer corps.

Almost all of the more senior parachute officers were drawn from the existing infantry units of the division or from the wider 'airborne family'. This was not altogether unreasonable, given the various technical aspects and requirements, but it also led inevitably to a degree of complacency and at least a lack of confidence in outsiders, if not actual suspicion of them. It had come as a surprise to many – not least to Brigadier Lathbury, who had been 'given to believe' that he would get the job – when Major General Urquhart was named as the new divisional commander.

Urquhart's appointment was, admittedly, something of a curiosity. In addition to a total lack of airborne experience, he was also prone to airsickness. He did have, however, an enviable track record as a combat commander and had led an independent brigade in North Africa with some success and flair. On the other hand, it is not clear that the Airborne Division actually needed a new commander at all. Urquhart's predecessor, Major General Eric Down, had been

General Urquhart and men of 1st Airborne Division.

dispatched eastward to form an Indian parachute division for operations against Japan, though there was no pressing need for such a formation – it would require many months of training and preparation before any Indian parachute or airborne units, still in their infancy, really required a combat commander. In effect, two men with extensive airborne experience had been passed over to make space for Urquhart, so it is only natural to wonder why and how this came about. The key word is patronage. Montgomery was much given to selecting protégés and then doing what he could to further their careers. This is not as unreasonable as it sounds since generals really do need to have subordinates that they can trust, men whose strengths and weaknesses they understand and on whose loyalty and efficiency they can count.

This – in the best of examples – is a mutually beneficial relationship. The subordinates learn the ways and habits of their superior and become expert in divining the difference between what the general wants to happen and the words in which he expresses his requirements. They also learn to adjust or even disregard instructions that are less than wise. It is, of course, a system that has a great many shortcomings. If the subordinates are always (or even usually) chosen on the basis of ability, the general ends up with a team of talented individuals who can work well together. But if the team is to be effective there has to be confidence that a disagreement or the pointing out of a flaw in a particular plan will not result in a sacking. The chief problem is that the general may surround himself with people that he likes to the exclusion of those with greater talent. Understandably, Montgomery was inclined to seek promotion for men he knew and who he considered to be of proven ability. One of these was General Horrocks, commander of XXX Corps, though at the time of the Arnhem operation he was far from well, having not yet fully recovered from serious wounds received in an air raid at Bizerte the previous year. He had replaced General Bucknall as commander of XXX Corps in August 1944 and had led his troops during a dashing advance through France after the German collapse following the battle of the 'Falaise pocket'. At one point his troops covered nearly 250 miles in six days – a remarkable achievement, though to some degree it was a matter of trying to keep up with the speed of the German retreat. Another of the protégés was Urquhart himself. When the decision – for whatever reason – was taken to replace Major General Down as the commander of 1st Airborne Division, Urquhart was Montgomery's candidate and Browning accepted him.

Down had been less than happy about the situation, which was not helped by the fact that his own posting to India and Urquhart's appointment were made in such a hurried fashion that he had no opportunity for a proper handover period, during which he could have given Urquhart some valuable guidance about the division as an institution. Instead, Urquhart had to take over most abruptly and to learn about the units under his command and the functions and practices of the formation from a standing start. The fact that he managed to do so, including establishing good relations with some very touchy individuals, is a testament to his qualities as a leader.

Although the functions of an airborne division are not, on the whole, radically different from any other infantry formation once it is on the ground, there are many aspects, often apparently quite minor, in practice. It would have been quite an achievement for anyone to really come to grips with this in a short period, and Urquhart only took formal command of the division on 10 January 1944 – though he had visited the headquarters of each of the brigades over the previous few days. Settling in to the appointment without the benefit of any useful interaction with his predecessor, he faced a process much harder than it should have been, although there were other considerations. In the early summer of 1944, Urquhart was put out of action with a bout of malaria, which kept him away from his duties for several weeks. During his absence, Brigadier Lathbury 'acted up' and took his place as the commander of the division, although that in turn removed Lathbury from his own primary role as commander of 1st Parachute Brigade. Urquhart was also seriously hampered by his problem with airsickness. As a rule he chose not to make use of the Oxford aircraft that had been supplied for his personal use, but instead had himself driven back and forth across the country to the units in his division and to the many conferences and planning sessions he had to attend in London and elsewhere. The former was unavoidable, but the latter used up many hours that could have been spent rather more profitably.

As if these problems were not enough, the division was not able to carry out the level or type of training that was really required. At the battalion level, individual units were able to undergo training on a reasonably regular basis – though serious shortcomings would become apparent in a number of units once battle was joined – but there was a near-dearth of brigade or divisional training. In a number of cases, Urquhart himself was clearly less than satisfied with the standard of readiness of units, even less happy about the practices and standards at brigade level and concerned that the division as a whole was not sufficiently open to suggestions from outside the airborne family. Given the fact that the intention was for the division to be deployed and to fight as a self-contained but integrated formation, this lack of training was a serious shortcoming that would have repercussions on the battlefield.

There were very real barriers to putting such training in place. Mounting a full-scale divisional or brigade exercise would give officers and men a valuable guide to many of the challenges they would face in action, but the costs would be enormous. Transport aircraft and their crews were in short supply at the best of times – not to mention the fuel requirements – and once the second front had been opened in June 1944 they were in even greater demand. Any losses incurred – and there would inevitably be damage to paratrooper transports and gliders even if none were actually irretrievably lost – would be hard to make good and there might well be loss of life in the event of an aircraft malfunction. There would be an additional strain on the ground crews, who were already overworked. There might also be an intelligence risk. Although allied security was remarkably effective virtually all the time, it would be difficult to find an area in Britain where many hundreds of aircraft could land an entire division without causing a stir of speculation and a chance that some word of the event might find its way to Germany. To some extent this could be balanced by carrying out training drops for individual units, or at least elements of units, but that was far from being the same thing as a divisional exercise – exactly the area where there was a serious deficiency. Neither of the parachute brigades conducted anything like as much formation training as they should have done through 1944, and much of what there was only involved portions of the brigades, or did not include a brigade parachute jump. This was in stark contrast to the Airlanding Brigade, which trained assiduously throughout the same period. Incredibly, there was only one divisional exercise, in the second week of May. Doubtless, lessons were learned, but the fact that the troops were committed to the field from trucks rather than from aircraft reduced the value of the exercise. A number of the men who landed in the Netherlands in September 1944 were struck by how well the process worked in the initial stages. At least two likened it to an exercise, although you have to question their basis for comparison since their experience of relevant exercises was so limited.

A further weakness that would become apparent once battle was joined was the nature of the divisional planning for the operation and also of brigade planning. Urquhart could not influence the chief problem – the distance to the target – but there were weaknesses in both the divisional plan and, most importantly, the plan for Lathbury's 1st Parachute Brigade. Some time after the operation, Lathbury himself suggested that it would have been wiser to retain one of his battalions as a brigade reserve and use it to reinforce whichever of the other two was making better progress, or possibly whichever encountered the greater resistance. It is perfectly possible that this would have been beneficial. A second battalion along either of the two more northerly routes might have been sufficient to overwhelm the forces of German commander SS Sturmbannführer Krafft. Alternatively, a second battalion, following Frost's men along the southern route, could have resulted in a much larger force at the bridge, which might have given at least a possibility that the objective could have been held for longer or even that both ends of the bridge might have been captured. The key words are 'could' and 'might'. It is equally possible that a second battalion on either of the northern routes would have resulted in nothing more than a longer column along a road being held up, while the head of the column struggled to deal with the German troops in its way, or that leaving one or other of the two northern routes unoccupied would have given the Germans better opportunities for disrupting the rest of the Airborne Division. It would certainly have taken some of the pressure off the German defences and even have allowed them to interpose forces between the units marching into Arnhem and the divisional area more quickly and more effectively than was the case.

In the hope of offsetting the distance problem, Urquhart decided to use his only mechanised combat unit – Major Gough's Reconnaissance Squadron – to make a rapid strike towards the bridge. The intention was that the majority of the squadron (less one troop, which would be retained as a divisional reserve) would overcome whatever resistance was in place and secure the bridge until the arrival of 1st Brigade. The squadron had no armoured vehicles, just jeeps. Each of these carried, as its main armament, a pair of Vickers 'K' guns that could, admittedly, deliver an enormous weight of fire. But they had no means of dealing with any sort of armoured vehicle, and since the men in the jeeps had no protection they would have to dismount, deploy and mount a conventional infantry-style attack on any force that blocked their way. As it turned out, the lack of an anti-tank capacity was not a significant factor since the squadron was prevented from carrying out its role by small-arms fire, but the presence of just one or two armoured cars or self-propelled guns which could cope with machine gun fire could easily have been enough to block their path. The concept of a surprise strike was not a bad one, but it was a very risky proposition without any form of armour. This need not have been an insuperable problem, since there actually was such a thing as a light tank – the Tetrarch – that could be transported by glider. Tetrarchs had not proved to be a great success in Normandy, where a small number were landed with 6th Airborne Division. However, they were never intended to face up to enemy tanks, but rather to provide a protected platform that could give close support to the infantry units and deal with light armoured vehicles such as armoured cars or armed half-tracks.

Major Gough was most unhappy about the role allotted to his unit; it was far from the purpose for which it had been designed. He proposed an alternative. His preference was that one troop from his squadron should be assigned to each of the battalions of 1st Brigade and that their task would be to locate the enemy and find alternative routes so that the battalions could avoid as much fighting as possible before reaching their objectives. Urquhart chose to reject Gough's suggestion and pressed on with the surprise attack concept. This would prove to be unfortunate twice over. If it had met no opposition at all, the squadron could have been on the objective within a matter of half an hour of leaving the landing zone – but making the assumption that that would be possible, let alone depending on it, was, at best, optimistic. After their first brush with the enemy, the Reconnaissance Squadron saw plenty of action, but very little in the specialist role for which it had been equipped and trained. Additionally, had a single troop of jeeps arrived at the bridge with or slightly ahead of Frost's battalion, they would have provided a major increase to the covering fire that could be provided for his attempts to secure the far end of the bridge through the night

A Vickers 'K' gun.

Members of the Reconnaissance Squadron.

of 17 September. In short, the experience of the Reconnaissance Squadron is a typical product of one of the major flaws in the planning process as a whole. Little consideration was given to the enemy and to how he might react to the arrival of a major parachute force on his doorstep, and it was virtually impossible to influence the senior staff once a decision had been made. There seems to have been a near-universal assumption that everything would be 'alright on the night'.

This questionable confidence extended beyond the vital issue of training for battle into equally significant areas – notably intelligence. The general tenor of the intelligence shared with the units was that the enemy would be thin on the ground and that his forces would consist largely of very young soldiers with limited training and experience, or old soldiers and invalids. There were, however, rather greater intelligence failures than that, and some at least could have been avoided. At least one can be laid firmly at the feet of General Browning. Whatever doubts he may have entertained, once he had made the decision that he would take his own headquarters to the battle, Browning was determined that nothing should get in the way of the operation going ahead. The fact that the airborne element of the operation would really take the form of three interdependent but essentially separate divisional actions – those of 82nd Airborne, 101st Airborne and the 1st Airborne with the 1st Polish Independent Brigade at Arnhem – meant that there would really be no genuine reason for Browning's 1st Airborne Corps Headquarters to leave Britain at all; there would be nothing of any value for them to do when they got there. He was set on having at least the appearance of a battlefield command and was quite prepared to traduce the reputation of a talented and conscientious officer along the way.

Shortly after the detailed planning for the operation commenced, an intelligence officer, Major Brian Urquhart (no relation to the general), became concerned about the possibility that the planning process was failing to make enough allowance for the German forces in and around the Arnhem area. He made arrangements for a reconnaissance sortie to examine the terrain and the results were profoundly disturbing. Photographs clearly revealed German armour within striking range of the landing zones and the town. Major Urquhart promptly arranged a meeting with Browning only to have his work dismissed – the photographs only showed a modest number of armoured vehicles, the vehicles were probably not fully operational, they might have been moved on to another location … and doubtless other observations along those lines. The net result was that no action of any kind was taken in relation to the operation, but Major Urquhart was packed off home on sick leave on the grounds that he was exhausted, although in reality he had been guilty of rocking the boat at a point when eagerness to get into the battle had overtaken sound judgement.

The Decision Process

By the end of the first week of September it was clear that some kind of intervention was required to regain the momentum of XXX Corps as the leading element of 2nd Army and thereby the main thrust of its parent formation, 21st Army Group. The delivery of an enormous airborne operation had the potential to do more than achieve a corridor through the Netherlands, which would enable the three corps of 2nd Army to deploy into Germany and threaten the German industrial base. Once the airborne troops were in action it was inevitable that the Germans would deploy every available unit against them. This would effectively prevent those assets from being committed against 2nd Army, which, rationally, would at least reduce the rate of the increasing resistance encountered by the British and put additional constraints on the plans of the German high command.

It might well have much greater consequences. Although the Germans were making a remarkably good job of reorganising their forces, their recovery from what had been a headlong retreat over several weeks was, at best, fragile. The arrival of a strong force behind German lines and the demonstration of sheer industrial and military power that was required to deliver the troops to the battle might well have brought about a degree of panic which would undo the efforts that had been partly responsible for making the Allied advance stutter and stall before the middle of September. It is impossible to gauge the extent to which this influenced Allied thinking, but it was undoubtedly a factor and not an unrealistic premise. The very process of diverting assets to meet the US and British forces at Eindhoven, Grave, Nijmegen and Arnhem would certainly disrupt the German supply chain and troops' transport arrangements, and it might well have a dramatic influence on the morale of the German Army as a whole. That does not imply that every unit in the army – or even a majority of them – was close to collapse, but the Germans were so heavily stretched that if even a modest number of units and formations disintegrated, surrendered or simply lost the will to fight, there were no assets to replace them and therefore units which continued to be effective might well have to be withdrawn for fear that they should become isolated. Even if every unit in the army stuck to its guns, the mere fact that there was a battle raging in their rear would inevitably cause them some concern at a time when morale was, in general, rather shaky.

Once the Market Garden concept had been adopted, it developed a certain momentum. It became very difficult for anyone to step out of line and point to flaws of any kind, although there were doubts about the efficiacy of the project. The commander of 2nd Army, General Dempsey – Montgomery's immediate subordinate and Horrocks' immediate superior – was not at all convinced that the airborne strike was the most suitable option. On 9 September he wrote:

It is clear that the enemy is bringing up all the reinforcements he can lay his hands on for the defence of the ALBERT canal and that he appreciates the importance of the area ARNHEM-NIJMEGEN. It looks as though he is going to do all that he can to hold it. This being the case, any question of a rapid advance to the north-east seems unlikely. Owing to our maintenance situation, we will not be in a position to fight a real battle for perhaps ten days or a fortnight. Are we right to direct Second Army to ARNHEM, or would we better to hold a LEFT flank along the ALBERT canal and strike due EAST to COLOGNE in conjunction with First Army?

(Lewis Golden, 1984)

Dempsey was in an excellent position to judge the situation and capabilities of 2nd Army; he had a good picture of the activity of the enemy and of the supply and manpower challenges facing his command. Additionally, he had extensive experience of the challenges posed in combined operations. In fact, that experience had been a factor in his appointment in the first place, so his belief that his troops could not fight a major battle for at least ten days should have carried plenty of weight, especially so bearing in mind that fifteen days from the date of the diary entry would cover the entire period of the Market Garden operation timetable.

Dempsey was not alone. Each of the three airborne divisional commanders had concerns, and a number of officers were less than confident – most famously General Sosabowski, who felt that this plan, like several other projects which had not been pursued, paid little heed to what the enemy might do. The lack of any serious consideration of the how effectively the German Army might react to the arrival of the airborne corps and the ground offensive was far from being the only problem with Market Garden, but it would certainly prove to be the most serious one. A problem that attends every form of policymaking – whether military, political or commercial – is that once the principal actors have made their decision, it becomes very difficult for their subordinates and advisors to challenge either the concept or the execution. For the subordinates there is a valid concern that they will be seen as rocking the boat at best or of being disloyal at worst. If their fears prove to be ungrounded they may be dismissed as scaremongers, and if they turn out to have been correct in their observations they may find that they have earned the distrust and resentment of their superiors. It is also a challenge for the principals, who, if they abandon a policy, may be seen, or see themselves, as lacking conviction. All too often, policymakers come to see any alteration to policy as a defeat; changing the policy simply because it is ill-considered becomes a weakness, so the plan itself becomes more important than the potential of the plan to bring success. The momentum of Market Garden achieved a critical mass very quickly because of its perceived strengths – the possibility of destabilising the German Army in north-west Europe, of liberating the Netherlands, of striking into Hitler's industrial base, of ending the V2 bombings and of bringing the war to an end by Christmas, not to mention bringing another three divisions into the battle which would be retained by 21st Army Group for the foreseeable future. By the middle of September the only things that could have definitively prevented Market Garden going ahead were unfavourable weather – which Montgomery had already been assured was very much less than likely – or the total collapse of the German forces in front of Horrocks' XXX Corps. The latter was not impossible, but the trend was clearly running in the opposite direction. The Germans were becoming more capable of resistance by the day. By 16 September the scene was set, the actors were at their opening positions and the curtain was about to rise.

Whatever the merits and demerits of the Market Garden plan, one important element was achieved in the initial stage of the operation. The Germans were undoubtedly taken by surprise. A few individuals had given some thought to the potential of an operation of this nature, and units – coincidentally in the Arnhem area – had undergone training to deal with an airborne attack, but there had been no serious consideration of the prospect and no specific contingency planning. When the first lifts of airborne troops arrived on their drop zones and landing zones, the Germans really were taken by surprise – though, as we shall see, that advantage was totally negated at Arnhem due to the distance between the landing zones and the objective.

The reaction to the offensive was, at every level, exemplary. Rather than simply adopting a crisis management approach, the Germans quickly assessed the situation and identified the strengths and opportunities of their position instead of focussing on the weaknesses and threats. The speed with which the Germans grasped the general concept of the Market Garden plan was not really that remarkable, though. Initially, Field Marshal Model thought that he might be the target of the operation himself, a conclusion that caused a rather hurried – and as it turned out sensible – abandoning of his headquarters, which was spread between the Tafelberg and Hartenstein Hotels in Oosterbeek. Model's reaction, though understandable, soon became redundant as the scale of the operation became apparent. There was clearly a much bigger project afoot. As soon as reports started to come in of the US landings at Eindhoven, along the road to Nijmegen, the intentions of the Allies were obvious. The target was clearly the capture of the series of river crossings that would enable the British to advance through the Netherlands, so the Germans took immediate steps to deny the bridges to the enemy and thus made rapid progress towards the business of frustrating the Allied plan. By the evening of the first day of the battle, the situation, if not quite under control, was certainly not anything like as dangerous as the Germans might have feared. There was every possibility that the Allies could be prevented from achieving their objectives at all, let alone in the time frame that Montgomery had envisaged.

It quickly became apparent to the Germans that the Arnhem force needed only to be contained. It was true that by the night of 17 September the Arnhem bridge was not under German control, but it was not really in British hands either. The Germans probably overestimated the size of the force at the bridge, but it was abundantly clear that only a modest proportion of 1st Airborne Division was present. The Germans could not be sure how large the force was, but clearly there was a significant number of British troops

The Tafelberg Hotel, Oosterbeek.

around the landing zones and more had been held up at locations in Arnhem itself. So long as the balance of the division was prevented from resupplying and reinforcing Frost's command, the bridge must eventually be recovered.

Preventing the Allies from relieving Frost along the road from Nijmegen was the real priority. In the short term at least, the battle being conducted between Arnhem and Oosterbeek was more a matter of containment than of destruction. Sheer good fortune had afforded the German command a major advantage. The two divisions of II SS Panzer Corps under Obergruppenführer Bittrich had been withdrawn from the battle after weeks of hard fighting in France and had concentrated in the Arnhem area as part of the process of refitting and reorganising. Both formations – 9th and 10th Divisions – had suffered heavy losses in manpower and equipment, but the surviving troops were exceptionally competent and well-motivated soldiers with a wealth of experience. A good deal has been made of the presence of II SS Panzer Corps, but it was not even close to its full combat strength. Additionally, it had been ordered to send any operational armoured vehicles back to Germany. This order had not been scrupulously observed and a number of vehicles had had weapons or other equipment removed to make them nominally unserviceable and had been retained.

Many of the German troops in the Arnhem area had been deployed in 'alarm' units of just a couple of dozen men and were scattered in penny packets throughout the region. This is generally seen as a precaution against parachute operations and would possibly have been effective at disrupting minor raids, although these units would clearly be valueless in the event of massive widespread airdrops. In fact their distribution would be a problem since they would have to be concentrated into larger units if they were to offer any viable opposition to a major force. The 'alarm' units are probably better seen as a deterrent to Dutch resistance activity and a means of showing the flag to the wider community, demonstrating and supporting the continued presence and power of the occupation government.

Although they had every reason to be confident that the Market Garden operation could be defeated, the Germans were not blind to the risks. Even if the Allies were prevented from reaching Arnhem and gaining a clear road all the way into the north of the Netherlands and Germany, any progress they might make would be presented in a positive light and would encourage the civilian populace in the occupied territories. The Allies might be left with a salient pointing to nowhere in particular, and expensive to maintain from attacks along its flanks, but that salient would effectively split the German defences and cause all sorts of problems of communication, resupply or the deployment of troops from one part of the front to another. Additionally, if the Allies were to be left with a forty or fifty mile salient to defend, the Germans would be obliged to line the flanks with units that could have been put to better use elsewhere. If the flanks of the salient were not contested, the divisions of 2nd Army would be able to fan out into the Netherlands unimpeded and the consequent gain in territory would be another propaganda coup for the Allies as well as being another blow to German confidence in the army – and at home – that there was any chance of even a temporary recovery, let alone a turn in the tide of the war.

On a strategic level, the analysts and planners in the German command structure were all too aware of the speed of the Allied onslaught after the Falaise battle. But they must have been equally conscious that the logistical demands on the rather tenuous transport network supporting that advance were enormous and that the effort could not be sustained indefinitely, or on every part of the front. They may well have been aware – unlike Bradley or Eisenhower – that General Patton's forces had secured considerable quantities of German fuel, but not how significant that might be in relation to the general's supply situation, though it would still be unlikely that Patton's army would have enough petrol to sustain the speed of advance indefinitely. It would have been reasonable to conclude that any major initiative by 21st Army Group would have consequences for Patton and that if his movements were curtailed in any way that would relieve some of the pressure on that part of the front. The US forces could hardly be ignored, but such resources as might become available could, if necessary, be committed to stopping 21st Army

Group and preventing Market Garden from being the breakthrough for which Montgomery and Eisenhower were looking.

Equipment

Delivering an airborne force clearly requires suitable transport – powered aircraft and, in most major operations of the Second World War, gliders. The glider-borne elements of 1st Airborne Division travelled to the Netherlands in mostly Horsa, but also Hamilcar, gliders, which were towed by the sixteen squadrons of 38 and 46 Groups of the RAF. The overwhelming majority of the parachute soldiers in Market Garden would jump from Dakota aircraft manufactured in the United States and provided by 9th Troop Transport Command of the USAAF. In 1944, US air units were assets of either the army, the navy or the Marine Corps; a separate air force had yet to come into being.

The Douglas C-47 Skytrain (known to the British as the Dakota) was a sturdy and reliable aircraft – so much so that a considerable number are still airworthy today. It did, however, have certain weaknesses. The lack of armament was not, as a rule, a significant issue since the transport aircraft would generally be protected by large numbers of fighters, but the Dakota did not have self-sealing fuel tanks or any protection for the cockpit, which made it vulnerable to any kind of anti-aircraft fire. With a cruising speed of 160mph and a range of 1,600 miles, the Dakota was an excellent paratroop aircraft, though it can hardly have provided a comfortable trip.

One portion of the British Airborne Division's paratroops jumped from converted Stirling bombers. The Stirling had, by this time, become obsolete in its original role, but had been pressed into service for the delivery of the first men on the ground – the pathfinders of 21st Independent Parachute Company. More Stirlings – and a number of other ageing bomber aircraft – were deployed as

General Urquhart disembarking from a Dakota.

tows for the gliders that would deliver the Airlanding Brigade and various elements of the parachute battalions, as well as the artillery, medical, engineering, service corps and other divisional assets.

The 7-ton Horsa had come into service in 1942. It was a very serviceable piece of equipment and somewhere between 4,000 and 5,000 would be built before production ceased. A Horsa could carry an airlanding infantry platoon of men, a jeep and trailer, a 6-pounder anti-tank gun or a 75mm Pack Howitzer. Assuming the Horsa made a good landing, a platoon of infantry or a vehicle could be unloaded quickly and efficiently, though extracting a jeep or gun required the entire tail section to be removed by means of quick-release bolts, which could be a problem if the glider did not come to a halt on the flat.

Some of the heavier equipment – notably Bren Carriers, the 17-pounder anti-tank gun and the Morris Tractors required to move them – called for the massive Hamilcar glider. With a wingspan of 110ft, it was actually a larger beast than the tow aircraft. The Hamilcar's cockpit, unlike that in the Horsa, was a bubble on top of the fuselage rather than at the nose, so if the glider turned over on

British paratroops en route.

6-pounder anti-tank gun at Oosterbeek.

landing the pilots were very likely to be crushed. All the same, the Hamilcar was an effective tool, and the majority of the guns and tractors they carried to Arnhem arrived safely – as did almost all of the Horsas.

There was, of course, a limit to the size and weight of burden that either the Horsas or Hamilcars could carry, so specific 'airborne' variants of several items had to be developed. Cut-down versions of

17-pounder anti-tank gun in the park behind the Hartenstein Hotel.

Unloading a Bren Carrier from a Hamilcar.

Morris Tractors, jeeps and 6-pounder guns were produced to fit the size and weight constraints of the gliders.

Having the necessary aircraft was one thing, ensuring that they could deliver their loads in the right locations was another. It was not impossible for a well-trained aircrew to identify a precise dropping zone by careful map reading, but it was certainly difficult. If the aircraft overshot the target by just two or three minutes, the glider

Airborne variant of the 6-pounder anti-tank gun.

An Airborne jeep after the battle.

Standard airborne jeep trailer – note the folding bicycle.

or paratroops might easily be two, three or four kilometres off target by the time they reached the ground. In the summer of 1942, the RAF had embarked on a programme to develop a beacon emitting a signal that would be received by a partner unit in one or more aircraft. These devices – the 'Eureka' broadcasting kit on the ground and the 'Rebecca' receiver on the aircraft – were designed to give the pilot a precise direction and distance to the drop or landing zone in time to alert the paratroops or glider pilot. The Eureka device was built with the valve technology of the day and would now be considered rather fragile compared to the solid-state electronics that we take for granted today. A single Eureka could provide a homing signal for up to forty aircraft, and the kits were used for a variety of operations, including the delivery of supply gliders to resistance movements and for the major airborne landings of 1944–5. Eureka was only part of the approach to site identification, though. Aircrews were still expected to apply normal navigational practice and also to watch out for coloured cloth panels, which would be spread on the ground to confirm the identity of specific areas within each drop zone or landing zone.

Specialist 'airborne' variants of items were produced for various reasons. The ordinary steel helmets issued to British infantry were impractical for either parachute or glider landings, as they did not have adequate padding against impact and had a rim that could easily inflict an injury on the wearer or his comrades. The troops were issued with the famous 'Denison Smock' – a camouflaged jacket designed by a Major Denison. This distinctive smock was more weatherproof than the usual British battledress and was, in most situations, a decent substitute for the army greatcoat. It was well provided with pockets and was both reasonably comfortable and popular – so much so that many officers and other ranks of non-airborne units went to some lengths to acquire them. The smock was originally intended to fit over the battledress and webbing, but experience soon showed this to be less than practical when trying to access the contents of the webbing pouches. It is clear from photographs of airborne troops in North Africa and Normandy as well as at Arnhem that many preferred to let out their webbing so that it could be worn over the smock instead of under it.

The majority of troops on both sides were armed with bolt-action rifles. For German soldiers this meant the 7.92 calibre Kar 98, the last in a line of Mauser-designed rifles that had been adopted as the standard weapon of the German Army in 1935. For the British it meant the Lee Enfield No. 4 .303, a remarkably accurate and reliable weapon – so much so that parts are still being manufactured in Pakistan. In 2011, a squad of US troops was kept pinned down for a whole day at a range of 700m by two Taliban fighters armed with aged No. 4 rifles.

Fine weapons as these were, they could not provide the kind of concentrations of small-arms fire that were frequently needed on the battlefield. Most non-commissioned officers on both sides, and a great many of the specialists in the airborne divisions, carried sub-machine guns – either the German MP 40 or the British Sten gun. Specialist 'airborne' versions of both weapons were developed. Each fulfilled the same role of providing concentrated bursts of bullets at short ranges. Although the Sten was generally seen as a second-rate weapon and was prone to jamming and other malfunctions, the later models were fairly reliable. A number of German soldiers discovered that a bit of work with a file could improve the Sten considerably and the guns were prized acquisitions for aficionados – in fact the Germans made several thousand Sten copies for issue to police force units in occupied countries.

Though the Sten gun's reputation for unreliability was not altogether unfair, it could be exaggerated. Brigadier Lathbury dropped his on the floor causing it to let off a burst that could easily have wounded or killed General Urquhart – Lathbury dismissed the Sten as being 'a temperamental weapon at best'. There were certainly issues with even the later designs. A report after the battle pointed out a weakness in the magazine spring that could prevent the rounds being delivered into the chamber of the gun. But for a weapon that had been designed in a great hurry in 1940, and specifically so that it could be made in factories and workshops with even the most basic facilities, the Sten was better than nothing at all and perhaps should enjoy a better reputation.

The MP 40 sub-machine gun was, overall, a more impressive item, and a good many were prized possessions of Allied soldiers who managed to 'win' one on the battlefield. It did have its weaknesses – the soldier had to keep it extremely clean and the projecting underslung magazine made it difficult to fire the gun effectively from a prone position.

The low weight, manoeuvrability and high rate of fire made both the Sten and the MP 40 vitally important elements in the infantry arsenal. At the sort of ranges typical of close fighting in built-up areas or woodland, they could be as effective, if not more so, as the light machine gun that provided the major source of firepower for German squads and British sections.

The British light machine gun – the Bren – was a development from the Czech ZB vz.26, the name 'Bren' being constructed from the first two letters of Brno – the city where the original weapon was designed and built – and Enfield in north London, where the British Army's model was manufactured. The Bren had many virtues: it was extremely reliable, relatively easy to maintain and very accurate – more so than was, perhaps, desirable in a light machine gun since the purpose is to give a tight spread of bullets in a small area, not to provide pin-point accuracy. It was light for a machine gun at only 22lb (10kg) and was generally popular with the troops. Prolonged fire – as with any other automatic weapon – could lead to overheating, which could damage the barrel and impair accuracy and reliability, although the barrel could be changed quickly by means of a single quick-release lever. The value of the Bren was somewhat compromised by the fact that it was magazine-fed and that the magazine held only thirty rounds – though experience had shown that in fact it was better to load only twenty-eight rounds to reduce a tendency to jam. Changing the magazine was straightforward, but it did mean that the weapon really needed a crew of two to provide a steady volume of fire. Although reliance on a magazine reduced the effective rate of fire in comparison with a belt-fed weapon, it did reduce ammunition expenditure by a considerable margin since the operator could not simply run off a belt of 100 or 150 rounds in a matter of seconds. A specific 'airborne' version of the Bren gun was designed in 1943 with a marginally shorter and lighter barrel, but it seems that a good many of the Brens taken to Arnhem and Oosterbeek were standard Mark I or Mark II models.

The Germans had started the war with the MG 34 light machine gun, primarily a belt-fed weapon, though several types of magazine were also available. It was an exceptional piece of design and proved to be reliable, accurate and, with a cyclic rate of fire in the region of 700 rounds per minute, frighteningly effective compared to the light machine guns of other armies. As well as being issued to infantry sections, the MG 34 was fitted to vehicles and fortified installations, and was the first true general-purpose machine gun. In theory, it had been superseded by the MG 42, which was more suitable for mass production, but the German factories were unable to meet the demand for the new gun and MG 34s continued to be used right up to the end of the war. Both weapons were sometimes referred to as 'Spandaus' by Allied troops, apparently a throwback to the German machine gun of the First World War that had been manufactured by the government arsenal in the Spandau area of Berlin.

Since both the MG 34 and the MG 42 could be used in a sustained-fire role, there was no direct German equivalent of the British Vickers machine gun. By 1944, the Vickers was already a venerable design. In 1915, a company of the Machine Gun Corps fired a million rounds in a 12-hour period without a single malfunction – though they did have to use 100 spare barrels to prevent overheating. The Vickers' remarkable dependability would keep it in use with the British Army into the 1960s.

In a conventional infantry division there would have been a machine-gun unit whose teams would have been allotted to individual battalions within the division as required, but in 1st Airborne Division each of the infantry battalions had a machine-gun platoon. A drawback of the Vickers machine gun was its weight. While the MG 34, the Bren and the MG 42 were all air-cooled, the barrel of a Vickers gun was encased in a jacket containing water and with a separate tank connected to the jacket by a short hose to allow circulation and dissipate heat. Once it had been put in position, the Vickers could be operated reasonably effectively by just two men – one to fire the gun and one to ensure a steady stream of belts of ammunition – although generally the team would actually comprise six to eight men to carry the weapon and an adequate supply of ammunition.

The standard Vickers gun was a rather different animal to the twin Vickers 'K' guns mounted on the jeeps of the Reconnaissance Squadron. The latter had a much higher rate of fire, and although it was most widely used as armament for aircraft it had proved itself as a vehicle-mounted weapon with the Long Range Desert Group in North Africa.

German MG 42 team. (Collection of David Smith)

The advent of the tank had changed the nature of combat radically and steps were taken from 1917 onwards to provide the infantryman with a weapon that could stop an armoured vehicle. Several countries developed anti-tank rifles – firing a high-velocity heavy-calibre bullet which, it was hoped, would penetrate the skin of a tank or armoured car and bounce around inside until it hit a crew member or caused some material damage to the inner workings of the vehicle. Anti-tank rifles were effective when a new concept and the tanks of the day were lightly armoured, but they were quickly made redundant by advances in tank design in the 1930s and 1940s. By 1944 they had been abandoned virtually everywhere and replaced by various forms of rocket or grenade launchers. The British weapon was the PIAT – or Projector, Infantry, Anti-tank weapon. With a range only slightly greater than 100yd, and of limited effectiveness against the heavier German tanks – the Panther and Tiger – the PIAT had a certain Heath-Robinson look about it, although it was fairly effective. There was little chance of penetrating the frontal armour of a Panther or Tiger tank, but the PIAT was quite capable of immobilising either of those vehicles with a hit to the tracks and running gear, and any lesser tank, armoured car or troop carrier could be utterly destroyed with a single round just as long as the operator could get a good clear shot at a close enough distance. To some degree the weapon's short range was offset by the fact that it could be fired safely from an enclosed space, unlike the US Bazooka or the German *Panzerschreck*, both of which produced a large back-blast of hot gas that could easily set a room on fire or cause severe injury to anyone who happened to be behind it, forcing the loader to duck away very smartly before the weapon was discharged. The German *Panzerfaust* was a much cheaper and lighter anti-tank alternative. A single-shot weapon, the widely issued *Panzerfaust* was an early form of rocket-propelled grenade.

All these anti-tank weapons had dangerously short ranges; by the time the target was close enough for the operator to open fire he would be at risk of being spotted and cut down by enemy infantry or the machine gun mounted on virtually every armoured vehicle. They could, however, all be put to an alternative use – blowing a hole through the wall of an enemy-held building. If the occupants were not killed they would very often beat a hasty retreat.

Infantry battalions in most, if not all, armies had some level of integral firepower that they could deploy immediately without having to rely on an artillery regiment in the vicinity that was not already engaged or committed to a fire plan. In British units the 3-inch and 2-inch mortars provided this firepower. When adopted by the British Army in the 1930s, the 3-inch mortar had a range of a little under a mile, but in the early stages of the war it soon became apparent that this was inadequate and new propellants were developed that increased the range to a more useful 2,800yd – roughly 2.5km. The whole assembly of tube, bipod and base plate weighed in at one hundredweight and could be carried by a team of three men for the mortar and another three to five to carry bombs. In general, however, the mortar platoon would need a Bren Carrier – or a jeep – to carry ammunition.

Fire support from the 3-inch mortar platoon could be called on as required, but platoon commanders could supply 2-inch mortars immediately. In some cases each section carried one of these light mortars to give a total of three for the platoon, but it was quite common to have only one or even to dispense with it entirely in favour of a PIAT or an extra Bren gun – there being a limit to the amount of ordnance soldiers can carry around.

The Gammon bomb – invented by Captain R. Gammon of the Parachute Regiment – was known officially as the No. 82 Grenade and consisted of a bag and a detonation device. The bag could be filled with a quantity of plastic explosive and any small hard objects such as stones, broken glass or empty cartridge cases that could inflict wounds on the enemy, or it could be stuffed with explosive for use against vehicles. The bomb was fitted with a length of ribbon and a small weight. The ribbon was kept in place by the weight until the bomb was thrown. It would then unwind from the bomb, keeping tension on the detonation mechanism in the air until it came to rest. Then the bomb would explode on contact with the target. Naturally the range was limited by the strength of the man throwing it, but it could be very effective, sending a fierce shockwave through any vehicle that received a hit. Gammon bombs were not generally issued to infantry units but were widely used by airborne troops and commandos.

The Hawkins (or No. 75) grenade was much more widely available and could be thrown at armoured vehicles or used as a mine. It was most likely to be effective in the latter role, when a number were spread across a road to cause an immediate explosion directly under the wheel or track of a passing vehicle. A Hawkins grenade was unlikely to destroy a medium or heavy tank, but it might well break a track and immobilise the vehicle.

Revolvers and automatic pistols were routinely issued to officers and specialists on both sides but were seldom of much practical value, though General Urquhart did (in the company of others) fire his at a German soldier who passed by a window, and there is a well-known photograph that shows a British officer with a pistol at a firing position in the Hartenstein Hotel at Oosterbeek. Most soldiers who were issued with a pistol, seem to have preferred to put their faith in a rifle or sub-machine gun as soon as one became available.

The only armoured vehicle deployed with the Airborne Division was the Bren Carrier. The Carrier was produced in massive quantities – more than 20,000 in total – and used for a wide range of purposes, from transporting mortars, machine guns and stores to casualty evacuation. A conventional infantry battalion would have a 'Carrier Platoon', which was designed to carry out reconnaissance tasks and provide a modest mobile reserve that could be deployed rapidly in virtually any terrain. Because of their considerable weight – a standard model weighed nearly 4 tons when fully loaded – only a small number of Bren Carriers could be taken to the Netherlands, to transport the 3-inch mortars and Vickers guns for each of the infantry battalions. These were not standard production models but variants reduced in weight by removing lockers, spares, a rear armour plate and various other parts, and built specifically for the airborne forces. The same process was applied to that ubiquitous Allied vehicle, the jeep. Every unit in the division had a number of these handy trucks – the Reconnaissance Squadron alone had thirty-two. With very modest alterations a jeep could be carried in a Horsa glider and extracted with relative ease and speed. To a great extent they took the place occupied by the Bren Carrier in conventional infantry battalions, carrying stores and casualties and as the prime mover for the 6-pounder anti-tank gun, the Polsten anti-aircraft gun and the 75mm Pack Howitzer. The Polsten was a lightweight and inexpensive version of the 20mm Oerlikon gun and was issued to provide a light anti-aircraft capability for airborne units. The 75mm Pack Howitzer was the principal armament of the 1st

Airlanding Light Regiment Royal Artillery. A US product, the howitzer weighed rather more than half a ton and could fire a shell weighing nearly 7kg to a maximum range of almost 8.5km. The gun itself – and the jeep to tow it – fitted well into a Horsa glider, but artillery ammunition took up a lot of space and could be expended at a prodigious rate. In total, the regiment required ninety gliders to deliver the unit headquarters and two batteries on the 17 September, with the remaining battery following in the second lift.

The lightweight 98cc Welbike motorcycle was designed to provide air-portable transport for agents and saboteurs dropped by parachute behind enemy lines (both the Germans and the Italians developed similar motorcycles), and also for rapid transport for dispatch riders in the battle area. The machine weighed a little over 70lb and had a range of about 90 miles on a single tank (less than 1 gallon) of petrol. The Welbikes were not the only two-wheeled transport available; a large number of folding bicycles were issued. A plan to tow strings

75mm pack Howitzer.

of cyclists behind motorbikes had a certain charm, but proved to be less than totally practical. Even when this was tried out on a large flat parade square it proved difficult to manoeuvre or halt without several of the cyclists falling to the ground.

Any sort of armoured vehicle was a major threat to airborne forces, and the Germans deployed whatever they could find as quickly as possible. The first armoured attacks on the western face of the airborne perimeter consisted of a company of French vehicles that had fallen to the Germans in 1940 but had long been relegated for training purposes. The airlanding units made short work of these, but the more modern armoured cars and tanks that were brought in as the battle progressed were much harder to deal with. The majority of the tanks were the Panzer IV model, which had given sterling service since its introduction before the start of the war, but was now showing its age. Even so, the design was very sound. Nearly 9,000 tanks were produced between 1936 and 1945, and a small number were still operational as late as 1967, seeing action in the Syrian army during the Six Day War against Israel. The Panzer IV had proved quite vulnerable to the PIAT and the US Bazooka, so a substantial number were fitted with armour plate 'skirts', pylon-mounted several inches away from the vehicle along the sides and around the turrets to make any projectile detonate against the skirt rather than the tank. Although German tank crews were, it seems, rather sceptical about the effectiveness of this additional armour, it did change the appearance of the Panzer IV and inexperienced Allied troops could sometimes mistake a Panzer IV for the much more heavily armed and armoured Mark I Tiger or Panzer VI. By 1944, the Mark I Tiger was being superseded by the Mark II, an even more heavily armoured monster – so large, in fact, that German crews found manoeuvring difficult in some of the narrow Arnhem streets.

Many of the armoured vehicles that the airborne force had to face were not, strictly speaking, tanks, but self-propelled artillery

A Welbike.

Folding bike strapped to a jeep.

or assault guns. Fully armoured and mounting a 75mm gun, these 'Stugs' – from the designation *Sturmgeschütz*, meaning assault guns – were built on the chassis of the Panzer III and then Panzer IV, but without a revolving turret, so the whole vehicle had to be turned to face the target.

One of the iconic vehicles of the Second World War was the German armoured half-track troop carrier known as the Hanomag. The title is widely used to cover an enormous range of vehicles produced for the German Army from 1939 to 1945. The primary role of the Hanomag was to transport a squad of infantry right up to – or on top of – enemy positions and to give the infantry a protected vehicle that could keep pace with tanks. Despite a total of more than 15,000 being produced, their supply was always at a premium. Earlier models had a large door in the rear of the superstructure to allow the occupants to de-bus under cover – at least from fire to the front – but in later models the squad had to simply jump over the side.

Destroyed 'Stug' assault gun.

This was less perilous than it might seem since the vehicle had a crew of two – a driver and a machine-gunner – who could keep up a sustained fire on the enemy while the infantrymen disembarked and advanced, or took up firing positions.

One of the most difficult things for 1st Airborne to deal with was not a weapon that had been designed for surface combat at all. The Germans equipped large numbers of half-track vehicles with anti-aircraft weaponry, ranging from 20mm cannon to twin or quadruple machine guns. These vehicles could obviously carry a great deal of ammunition and were used to great effect in pinning down troops trying to make their way to the bridge and in support of counter-attacks. On most models, the crew were somewhat vulnerable to small-arms fire, though some were enclosed to varying degrees and could only really be dealt with by anti-tank weapons.

The two defining markers of the Airborne Division are the Denison smock and the famous 'Red Beret', though it is actually

'Stug' self-propelled gun.

A Hanomag in action.

German Hanomag armoured troop carrier.

maroon. Photographs of the battle indicate that the men found the smock to be practical and there are very few pictures of men without one. The beret, on the other hand, seems to have been less common on the battlefield than romance would indicate – presumably on the practical grounds that a steel helmet may not offer much protection from a bullet but it is a good deal better at keeping out both shrapnel and rainfall than a cloth beret. It is also easier to apply camouflage to a helmet, especially one fitted with a net designed for that very purpose – not to mention the fact that maroon is not a particularly good colour when it comes to blending into the landscape. Some men certainly did discard their helmet in favour of the beret, but common sense – as well as the photographic record – would suggest that they were in the minority.

Relatively few photographs show German infantry soldiers in anything other than the characteristic coal-scuttle helmet in the battle, though some are so heavily festooned with foliage that they are hard to identify, which is of course the object of having a camouflage net. Although many designs of camouflage smocks were produced for both the *Wehrmacht* and the SS, there were never really enough to go around, so between the shortages, the fact that new designs were introduced before the old one could be made universal and also because units were hastily assembled out of whatever manpower could be found, photographs of German soldiers at Arnhem tend to

Red beret found near Oosterbeek church. (Courtesy of Philip Reinders)

show a wide variety of clothing and equipment. One of the items that occurs most frequently is the well-known cylindrical gas-mask case. In reality, no one expected gas attacks by 1944, but they were obviously useful containers – otherwise infantrymen would not have carried them about.

3

D-DAY: SUNDAY 17 SEPTEMBER

There was a good deal of activity in the sky over Arnhem, Ede, Wolfheze and Oosterbeek for some time before the arrival of the transport airlifts. Throughout the early part of the day, fifty Mosquito fighter-bombers and seventy-two Boston and Mitchell bombers conducted raids on German barracks and installations in the Arnhem–Nijmegen–Ede area, including a strike on the psychiatric hospital at Wolfheze, which, it was believed, was the location of a German headquarters unit.

The journey was largely uneventful, but Urquhart was probably not the only person to feel reassured by the sight of assorted rescue craft under the flight path. Despite a brief encounter with a force of fifteen German fighters, remarkably few aircraft failed to arrive over the Netherlands and very few of them dropped their paratroops or released their gliders in the wrong location.

The German pilots must have been astonished at the enormous quantity of aircraft en route for the Netherlands. In addition to massive numbers of transports and gliders, there were something in the region of 1,200 fighter aircraft protecting the convoy, while yet more – notably long-range fighters on bomber sector sorties – attacked targets throughout the area.

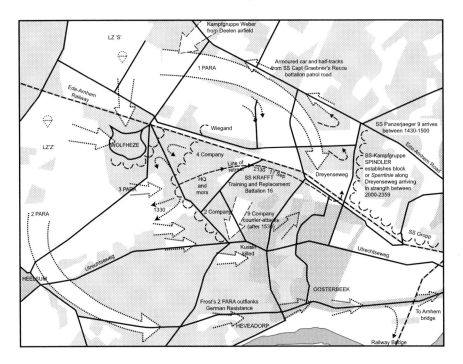

Progress of the battle on 17 September.

Urquhart's Horsa was piloted by Lieutenant Colonel Ian Murray, commanding officer of one of the two 'wings' (effectively, the equivalent of battalions in British military parlance) of the Glider Pilot Regiment. Urquhart shared the trip with his batman, Private Hancock, and a jeep and suffered somewhat from the airsickness that he had experienced on all his flights. His glider made a good landing, though he witnessed one of the Hamilcars turning upside down, which was likely to have resulted in injury, if not death, for the two pilots in their bubble canopy on top of the glider.

The divisional war diary for 17 September is remarkably brief and exudes a degree of confidence. It records the departure of the Independent Company at 1015 hours (military time) and of the balance of the first lift thereafter, and has nothing to say about the journey to the Netherlands, largely because there was little to say. The diary entries (see the Pegasus Archive website) record the arrival of the glider-borne elements – divisional troops and 1st Airlanding Brigade –

at 1300 and the 1st Parachute Brigade drop at 1440, and that flak (anti-aircraft fire) had been slight. Divisional Headquarters was established to the south-west of Wolfheze at 1415 and the General Officer Commanding (GOC), Urquhart, left his headquarters at 1630 to visit Hicks' 1st Airlanding Brigade and thereafter Lathbury's 1st Parachute Brigade. This was a reasonable record of events to that point, but the final entry for the day at 1900 stated that operations were proceeding according to plan, which was far from correct. In fact, although the diary does not explicitly say so, a major problem had already been encountered. The fact that Urquhart had to leave his headquarters to find out what was happening in the Airlanding Brigade areaas and Parachute Brigade is a clear indication that communication had not been established between Urquhart and the two combat formations. This was not unusual and, as we know now, the soil conditions in the area would hamper the wireless equipment throughout the operation – but things had started to go badly wrong long before 1900.

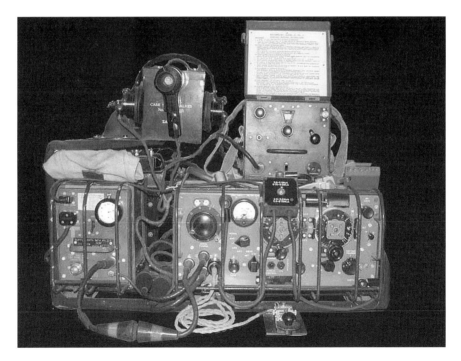

No. 22 wireless set. (Courtesy of Philip Reinders)

The drop and the glider landings had, in fact, run very well indeed – much better than most people would have expected or even hoped. Although generally thought of as single entities, the dropping and landing zones were actually divided into four dropping zones (DZs) for paratroops and five landing zones (LZs) for gliders to try to have each unit land in as small an area as possible to ease the process of concentrating the men of each company, squadron and battalion before they set off to their allotted destination. The first unit on the ground arrived 20 minutes ahead of the first wave of gliders. The task of the 186 officers and men of Major Wilson's 21st Independent Parachute Company was to overcome any resistance in the immediate vicinity of the LZs and DZs. Little resistance was expected. This was a perfectly reasonable assumption since the zones themselves were obviously not of any military significance and there was no reason for the German Army to have any presence at any of them. This turned out to be quite correct and Major Wilson's men encountered only a handful of stray Germans, who either took to their heels or were killed or captured as the company set about its mission of marking out the separate zones with crimson and orange recognition panels and smoke, and setting up the Eureka equipment. This was the company's first jump from Stirling bombers rather than Dakotas or Whitleys and the change in transport aircraft required some reorganisation of the individual 'sticks' (the term for the body of men in each aircraft). Number 1 Platoon carried out the site identification process on DZ 'X' for 1st Parachute Brigade. Number 1 section was assigned to laying out identification panels, operating the Eureka equipment and laying smoke to indicate wind strength and direction, though each section carried the required equipment to ensure that if one section were lost – which might easily happen through aircraft failure, enemy action or simply by being dropped at the wrong location – the pathfinding task could still be discharged.

Number 2 Platoon was assigned to LZ 'Z' to mark out the area for the arrival of 1st Brigade's glider-borne support elements,

British paratroops with a prisoner.

including an anti-tank gun battery, 16 Parachute Field Ambulance and 1st Parachute Squadron Royal Engineers. These two zones were adjacent to one another and separated by about 1km from LZ 'S' to the north of Wolfheze, where 21st Independent Parachute Company Headquarters and No. 3 Platoon marked out the area in which 1st Airlanding Brigade would arrive. All of these tasks were carried out effectively and with the loss of only one man – Corporal James Jones – who had the misfortune to be accidentally shot in the head shortly after landing and was thus almost certainly the first battlefield casualty of the Market Garden operation. With its first day's objectives completed with total success, the Independent Company made its way to Reijerscamp and formed a defensive position for the night.

The Independent Company had carried out its duties with great efficiency. The forty-eight gliders (eight had not completed the journey) carrying the King's Own Scottish Borderers had been released 2 miles from their LZ, and carried out their landing and rendezvous drills in short order. One man had been killed and one of the anti-tank guns damaged beyond immediate repair, while two others had been in gliders that had aborted or crashed as had some of the mortars and Vickers machine guns. The battalion, though, was able to start moving off at about 1500 to its planned positions at the drop zone arranged for 4th Brigade the following day. Once there, they set about digging in – a process that their chaplain, Captain Morrison, would later remark was a much easier business in the soft soil of the Netherlands than it had been on exercises on the chalky landscape of Salisbury Plain.

Urquhart does not seem to have designated line of succession until the morning of 17 September and did so only to his chief of staff, Lieutenant Colonel Charles Mackenzie, not to the officers concerned – a matter that would cause some difficulty and ill-feeling on the Monday. The situation would have been very difficult

Glider landing zone.

indeed if Mackenzie and Urquhart had both been lost or delayed in the early stages of the battle, which could easily have occurred. Aircraft failure could have held up either or both of them in southern England for some hours, they might have crashed or been shot down or premature glider release might have left either or both of them miles away from the battle.

The LZ where Urquhart landed was secure and filled with men unpacking vehicles, guns and stores. Some years later he wrote that it was just like being on an 'exercise in Hampshire'. This seems to have been the picture – other observers made very similar observations – which possibly gave an unrealistic air to the proceedings, an impression that the whole division would be able to march to Arnhem unimpeded by the enemy. If so, it was an impression that was not going to last for long.

The war diary of 1st Airlanding Brigade Headquarters – in common with several other units – had to be compiled after the operation due to the loss of the intelligence officer who had responsibility for the document. Some information was lost and some minor details may be in conflict with material recorded in other unit diaries or in personal accounts. This issue applies to much, if not all, of the Arnhem Oosterbeek source material. The brigade headquarters was on the ground by 1315 and gathered at its rendezvous in the middle of LZ 'S'. The South Staffordshires cleared the village of Wolfheze then moved off to Reijerscamp, leaving elements of the Glider Pilot Regiment to hold the village and control the railway line. The brigade's Main Dressing Station (MDS) was established near Brigadier Hicks' Headquarters in Wolfheze. With the Border Regiment and the King's Own Scottish Borderers guarding the LZs and DZs, the brigade had fulfilled its initial responsibilities and the units had dug in to await the second lift.

Urquhart watched the landings and then, as men wrestled an anti-tank gun through the side wall of a smashed glider, made his way across the fields to where 1st Brigade made its jump less than a quarter of a mile away. Almost all the 'sticks' were closely concentrated and Urquhart could see that the assembly of 1st Brigade was quick and efficient. By 1500, all three of the battalions had made their rendezvous, and both 2nd and 3rd Battalions were moving off the LZs, followed by 1st Battalion some time later. Lieutenant Colonel Dobie had not been impressed with the role assigned to 1st Battalion, and his intelligence officer, Lieutenant V.A. Britneff, would later complain that the battalion had had to 'hang around for an hour' on the drop zone before receiving permission to move off – a considerable delay given the fact that the element of surprise had already been seriously compromised. Aware that the vital task was to get to his objective with his battalion intact and not to fight a series of actions against whatever German forces he met along the way, Colonel Dobie decided to take a slightly different route in the hope of finding the course of least resistance. His orders had made allowance for this, but one of his companies had to fight its way through woods until it found the Amsterdamseweg road, where its advance was barred by a strong force – and there the company remained until dusk. With his companies now separated (unusually, the rifle companies of 1st Battalion were identified as 'R', 'S' and 'T' rather than the more traditional 'A', 'B' and 'C'), and with 'R' company well behind the main column of the battalion, Dobie decided to load all of the battalion's jeeps with the wounded men, send them back to find a dressing station and then pick up 'R' company and rejoin the battalion as quickly as possible. No sooner had this been set in motion than Dobie received a wireless communication from Lieutenant Colonel Frost at the bridge, to the effect that he had reached the objective and needed whatever help he could get. Dobie now decided that he had to make all speed to join Frost. Clearly, fighting through the woods was not helping the situation so the battalion now set off in a south-easterly direction to try to pass by the left flank of the German force that stood to its front. In an effort to deceive the enemy, all the battalion's transport was to be manhandled – a difficult undertaking – and the battalion spent the night trying to reach the lower road by way of the Stationsweg through Oosterbeek.

The Reconnaissance Squadron was delayed for a short while and did not start its move to Arnhem until around 1530. Progress, though, was short-lived. Within 15 minutes or so the squadron was stopped by enemy resistance on the track running on the north side of the railway line. While this action was under way, Gough – the squadron commander – received orders to find General Urquhart, who was anxious to launch the Reconnaissance Squadron on a different approach to the objective. Urquhart's message had not been relayed to Gough as speedily as it might have been since the squadron was operating on the 1st Parachute Brigade's wireless net rather that the divisional system. This was understandable since the squadron had been placed under Lathbury's command for the day, but Gough was now compromised by the fact that he could not raise the divisional commander – or his headquarters – by radio and was obliged to try and find him in person. He spent some time chasing about the divisional area, such as it was, trying to locate Urquhart – at one point he nearly drove right into a German position and was only prevented from doing so by the intervention of Major Dennis Mumford, commander of 3rd Battery of the 1st Airlanding Light Regiment Royal Artillery. Having failed to find Urquhart, Gough eventually located the tail end of Lathbury's Brigade Headquarters, where he learned that both Lathbury and Urquhart were moving with 3rd Battalion and that the plan was now for Gough's squadron to make its way to the bridge. He had no means, however, of passing that instruction to the squadron so he asked 1st Brigade Headquarters signallers to pass the order on to the squadron at the earliest opportunity and decided that the best thing he could do was to press on to the bridge himself.

For whatever reason, this plan did not find its way to the balance of the squadron, and Gough would now be separated from his command for the rest of the battle. In practice, there has to be some doubt over whether this really made any difference to the situation. The reconnaissance jeeps were capable of delivering an enormous concentration of small arms fire and might well be able to dispose of enemy infantry, but they had very little capacity for dealing with even the lightest of armoured vehicles. With nothing more effective than PIATs the troops would have had to dismount, deploy and then stalk any armoured car, self-propelled gun or tank that barred their way, while very vulnerable to small arms fire themselves, as the brief action north of the railway line had already demonstrated.

By the latter part of the afternoon, the plan to seize the bridge with a mobile force had already failed. It had always been the case that the brigade would have to reach its objectives on foot, and clearly that would take at least 3 hours, even if there were no enemy activity. But if the operation was to be successful, the brigade would now have to make a rapid march throughout the afternoon with no advance knowledge of the activity of the enemy and then eliminate whatever resistance they encountered in order to obtain the objectives.

Although the drop itself had run smoothly, the situation was now not looking very promising. Within a short space of time, Urquhart's tactical headquarters was up and running and the first piece of bad news had become apparent. The signals situation was far from satisfactory. Urquhart had seen 1st Parachute Brigade preparing to get under way, but he had no information about the situation of the Airlanding Brigade on the far side of the railway line to the north. Accordingly, he got in his jeep and was driven to Hicks' Headquarters, where he found that the brigadier was not present but out among the battalions of his command. Urquhart did, however, learn that the brigade had had a good landing and was setting about its tasks.

The South Staffordshires – missing two of its companies, which had been rescheduled for the second lift due to the shortage of gliders and towing aircraft – took up positions at Reijerscamp to protect LZ 'S' and the Border Regiment deployed north of Heelsum and Renkum to secure LZs 'X' and 'Z'. The King's Own Scottish Borderers and 1st Airlanding Brigade Headquarters moved off to the north and west to ensure the safety of DZ 'Y', where 4th Parachute Brigade was scheduled to arrive the following day. A party of Dutch SS troops arrived at DZ 'Y' at around 1500 but were quickly disposed of by the Borderers, as was a second foray about 2 hours after dark. An attempt to disrupt the landing areas by an enemy scratch force of about ninety men from Deelen airfield was given short shrift by the South Staffordshires, but beyond that there was little activity in the Airlanding Brigade's area throughout the day, though the commander of the NCO school at Schoonerewoerd – *Standartenführer* Hans Lippert – was ordered to move his unit to Renkum and engage the British troops there. The NCO school consisted of experienced and well-motivated soldiers, but clearly there were not enough of them to deal with a determined force, so they were reinforced with two units, each of several hundred men. One of these consisted of Luftwaffe personnel and the other of naval men, but neither group had received any infantry training worthy of the name and were of little value to Lippert or his veterans.

The initial stage of the operation – getting the air fleet to the Netherlands and then getting the men on to the ground – had gone remarkably well; if anything it had gone better than the information supplied to Urquhart indicated. On arriving at Hicks' Headquarters, he was told that a large proportion of the Reconnaissance Squadron's jeeps had failed to arrive, though this was not the case – in fact, almost all of Major Gough's squadron had landed successfully. Though untrue, the report had two major consequences. The plan for the Reconnaissance Squadron to act as a surprise force was now thought to be impractical, and Brigadier Lathbury needed to be informed that one of his three battalions would have to make good speed through Oosterbeek and Arnhem and in all probability fight for and hold the main objective itself.

On his return to his own headquarters Urquhart was made aware that there was still no signals link to 1st Parachute Brigade. The original plan had allotted one troop of the Reconnaissance Squadron as a divisional asset, and Urquhart now wanted that troop to ensure that he had a clear route to Lathbury. He could not, however, find either the troop in question or Major Gough, who, in turn, was trying to find Urquhart. Aware that Lathbury's headquarters could not be all that far away, Urquhart decided to forgo the protection of the troop of reconnaissance jeeps that had been assigned to Divisional Headquarters for just that sort of task and went to take a look at the situation for himself. Before he left, he gave orders that Gough should now meet him at Lathbury's Headquarters and then make his way into the town. Urquhart headed south for the 'Lion' route allotted to Frost's 2nd Battalion and followed it until he found the tail end of the column between Oosterbeek and Arnhem. Urquhart found Lieutenant Colonel Frost's Headquarters, but not the man himself, who was directing the leading elements of his battalion in their efforts to deal with a German armoured car.

Urquhart had been struck by the nature of the terrain. There is a tendency to think of the Netherlands as being completely flat, but contour maps can be misleading. Small depressions or slopes in the landscape that do not register at all on a map can be more than large enough to hide soldiers and vehicles or simply to prevent anyone from seeing further than 100–200 metres. He had also been surprised by the widespread use of wire chain fencing in residential areas, which might well present problems for his advancing troops. Most significantly, he was struck by the feeling that the column was moving very slowly. Rather than create another distraction for Frost, Urquhart left a message that he hoped would get Frost to move his battalion rather more quickly and then headed off once again in search of Lathbury, who, he was informed, was with Colonel Fitch's 3rd Battalion on the central 'Tiger' route.

Urquhart found 3rd Battalion was less than halfway to the centre of Arnhem and under fire at a road junction in woodland. He also saw a wrecked German staff car and the body of major general Kussin, the Arnhem town commandant. A number of units laid claim to the ambush that killed the major general – 9th Field Company Royal Engineers and the Reconnaissance Squadron being just two – though it seems most likely that it was in fact men of 3rd Parachute Battalion. Kussin had been killed trying to make his way back to his own headquarters, despite the strong advice of SS Sturmbannführer Krafft of 16th Panzer Grenadier Depot and Reserve Battalion – a unit whose determined actions would have an enormous impact on the first day of the battle. Kussin's body lay in the road until the next day, when Captain Pare – chaplain to No. 1 Wing of the Glider Pilot Regiment and attached units – enlisted the help of two German prisoners to help bury the unfortunate Major General and his fellow-passengers.

The progress of Lieutenant Colonel Fitch's 3rd Battalion had been slower than that of 2nd Battalion due to the heavier degree of resistance. There had not been a major engagement, rather a succession of minor fire fights or just the odd isolated round fired from cover, but each incident resulting in the loss of another one, two, three or more men. The overall strength of the battalion was not greatly affected, but the time it took to dislodge each German position was having a disastrous effect on the timetable, and efforts to find a better route did not yield results. At one point Fitch decided to send his 'C' Company on a flanking move, leaving the Utrechtseweg and moving along Breedelaan in search of a path of less resistance. The premise was sound, but 'C' company found themselves in an extensive fire fight in close country, not on a better path into Arnhem, though ten men would eventually manage to reach the bridge.

Meanwhile, the German commanders had not been simply watching events to see what would transpire; they were determined to seize and retain the initiative. The commanding general of both the western front (*Oberbefehlshaber* West or 'OB West') and of Army Group B (the forces facing the Allies in the north of Europe) was Field Marshal Walter Model. He had been in his post for only a few weeks. His predecessor, General von Kluge, had held the post for only a month and had been relieved during the retreat across France. Model had recently set up his headquarters in a small Netherlands town with no particular military significance but which had good communications in all directions – Oosterbeek. When the news of the airborne force arrived, he initially thought it quite possible that this was a raid to neutralise the only target of military value in the vicinity – himself. This was not an unreasonable reaction. Missions to capture or kill key commanders were not unknown, so Model and his staff made a hasty exit, leaving a quantity of personal effects and piles of administrative documents. Their evacuation was so hasty that when airborne troops arrived at the Hartenstein Hotel (Model himself had been staying at the nearby Tafelberg Hotel) they found the dining table set for lunch and promptly started helping themselves until they were encouraged to continue with their march.

The sheer size of the force had quickly disabused Model of the idea that he was the target, and he promptly drove off to the headquarters of the nearest formation of any note – II SS Panzer Corps at Doetinchem – to construct a response. The commander of II SS Panzer Corps, Obergruppenführer Wilhelm Bittrich, received news of the landings at Arnhem and Nijmegen from the Luftwaffe and made the correct deduction that Montgomery was trying to seize a road that could carry his army right across the Netherlands and on into Germany. He was impressed but not overawed and took what were really fairly obvious steps to prevent the operation from being Montgomery's hoped-for success. Both of Bittrich's divisions had been badly weakened in the battles in France, but he ordered them straight into action. His 9th SS Panzer Division, known as the Hohenstaufen, was given instructions to occupy Arnhem and defeat the forces to the west of the town, while the other – 10th SS Panzer, Frundsberg – was to set off to Nijmegen and secure the river crossings there. Bittrich had understood Montgomery's plan and saw that if the Nijmegen bridges could be kept out of enemy hands the Arnhem bridges would be an irrelevance. General Sosabowski had made the point that if the potential of Arnhem was obvious to the Allies and the potential for a thrust through the Netherlands so significant, there was surely a good chance that it was equally obvious to the Germans. As usual, he had been quite right and – as usual – he had been ignored. By the time Urquhart had made contact with his troops marching toward Arnhem, the Germans were already taking action.

From an early stage, the slow pace of the advance had frustrated Urquhart, but to begin with he was not too concerned about the overall situation. His analysis was that the units of 1st Brigade were meeting modest opposition, which was certainly slowing things down, but not enough to risk endangering the operation as a whole. Like Urquhart, Lathbury was unhappy at the rate of progress and the fact that he did not have effective communication with Frost's 2nd Battalion on the 'Lion' route to the south and had had no contact whatsoever with 1st Battalion on the 'Leopard' route to the north. The remaining battalion had been in intermittent contact with the enemy, and as daylight slipped away it had become bogged down less than halfway to its objective.

If Lathbury felt that he was not able to influence the battle, then Urquhart was in the same boat. He considered returning to his headquarters, but that was out of the question because, although 3rd Battalion had marched along the Utrechtseweg just a few hours before, there was no guarantee that the road would still be free of German troops. In Urquhart's view, he did at least have the advantage of being with the brigade that was leading the fight, and there was probably very little more he could do if he were at his own headquarters. Not long after dark, when it became clear that 3rd Battalion was not going to make any progress, Lathbury and Fitch agreed to halt for the night and resume the advance in the morning.

This was a curious decision, to say the least. Lathbury was aware of the situation at the bridge as he had been in contact with his brigade headquarters, and he also knew that the lower route to Arnhem – the one taken by Frost's battalion – had been clear of the enemy just a short while before and that there was no reason to think that any major force had entered the area. It is extremely hard to see any justification at all for Lathbury's course of action. It is certainly true that a portion of Fitch's battalion had not yet caught up with the leading elements, but the addition of even a modest force to the body of troops at the bridge should have been uppermost in his thinking. Failure to move on as quickly as possible would give the Germans a greater opportunity to take steps to prevent any further contact with Frost's command and to organise a blocking force or even a counter-attack that might well keep Fitch's battalion right where it was – in the vicinity of the Hartenstein Hotel. The decision

General Urquhart behind the Hartenstein Hotel.

was not universally welcomed; Major Anthony Hibbert, Brigade Major to Lathbury's brigade, urged him to press on to the lower road, but to no effect. There is no way of ascertaining whether doing so would have had any real benefit. There was every possibility that 3rd Battalion would have become scattered and disorganised during a night march, and although the road had been clear just a short while before, Lathbury could not be confident that this was still the case. Even a relatively small force – especially if it were handled effectively – could be enough to hold up the advance through the hours of darkness, in which case Lathbury might find himself and the battalion in an extremely vulnerable situation by dawn. Alternatively, he might just as easily have established an open road to the centre of Arnhem and been able to join the troops at the bridge with a significant force and put himself where he ought to have been – at the centre of the battle and with his brigade headquarters. The mere fact of getting 3rd Battalion to the bridge would not have guaranteed that the lower road could have been kept open for further additions of men or stores, but failure to do so certainly gave the Germans an opportunity to bar that route. As it was, there was no means of making the lower road an easy passage; German troops were firmly ensconced on the far bank of the river and would be able to impede, if not actually prevent, any troop movements toward the objective. The force at Lathbury's disposal was certainly not strong enough to cover the whole route from Oosterbeek to Arnhem, so even if he had ordered Fitch to continue the advance he might have achieved no more than having a somewhat larger force cut off at the bridge. It is not clear exactly what Lathbury had in mind on the night of 17 September, but there is a strong possibility that he had concluded that the purpose of the operation would be best served by a fresh attack by both 1st and 3rd Battalions at first light and that his force would be bolstered by the arrival of the second lift, which would not only bring more troops into the battle but very likely oblige the German command to commit any reinforcements to attacking the landing zones rather than to preventing his advance to the bridge. If so, he was being somewhat optimistic. The Germans were well aware of the intent of the operation and would therefore be focussed on preventing the airborne troops from achieving their chief objective. Without the Arnhem bridge, the Airborne Division was no more than a body of troops contained and under pressure on the north bank of the Neder Rijn and highly vulnerable to armoured attacks and artillery concentrations. Until such time as the British actually secured the bridge, they would not be that much of a threat, and therefore the German high command would be able to concentrate its attention on preventing the timely advance of XXX Corps. So long as the British were able to deny use of the bridge, they would be an inconvenience but not much more than that. It was certainly time-consuming to send units to block the routes around Nijmegen by alternative paths, but it was not an insuperable problem.

In fact, by late afternoon on 17 September, the whole airborne plan had been compromised. A complete set of orders was found

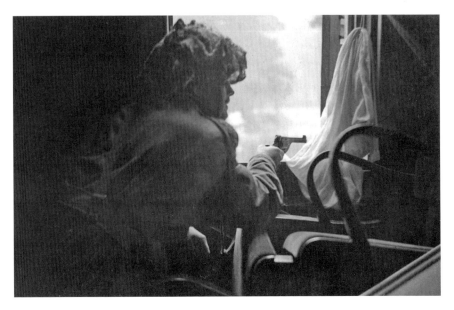

Defending the Hartenstein Hotel.

on the body of a soldier whose glider had been shot down. Since the airborne part of the operation was now fully revealed – Model had it in his hands by about 1700 – deducing the intentions of General Horrocks' XXX Corps was hardly an intellectual challenge. Allowing the Germans access to the plan was a professional failure on a huge scale, but it is hard to see that it really made a great deal of difference. Surprise had been forfeited by dropping the troops so far from their objectives, but the principle intention of Market Garden must have been glaringly obvious as soon as it was evident that the forces involved were so great that they could not possibly be mere raiding parties.

The only possible objective for the operation was to secure a road through the Netherlands, and clearly the only possible response for the Germans was to ensure that that did not happen. Bittrich – a very experienced and competent officer – must have been surprised at the audacity of the operation, but does not seem to have been overly concerned about the challenge facing his troops. Talking with his staff he is reported as saying, '… the British soldier will not act on his own initiative when he is fighting in the town and it becomes more difficult for officers to exercise control. He will be incredible in defence, but we need not be afraid of his offensive capabilities' (Robert Urquhart, 1958). Broadly speaking, Bittrich's analysis would prove to be soundly based, but on the afternoon of 17 September Urquhart's troops were making progress – though not as quickly as he would have liked. At dusk, Frost's men – having seen the railway bridge blow up in their faces –had secured half of the main objective, but the rest of 1st Brigade were held up in the town. The battle was going badly, but to the men of the Airborne Division it was certainly not lost and it probably would not have seemed so to General Urquhart had he been at his headquarters. But he was not there; he was in an attic in Arnhem surrounded by German troops.

4

D+1: MONDAY 18 SEPTEMBER

According to the divisional diary entry at 0600, operations had 'developed according to plan', though really this was far from true. Only one battalion of 1st Brigade had reached its objective; the other two had 'encountered stiff resistance on roads leading into Arnhem' (Divisional Headquarters Diary, Pegasus Archive). This was something of an understatement, although that may not have been clear to the officer compiling the diary. All the same, the failure to secure 1st Brigade's objectives in the course of the first day of the battle did not bode well. Throughout the morning, three references were recorded to the absence of General Urquhart – at 0700 and 0900 the diarist mentioned that it had not been possible to raise him on the wireless net and then, at 0915, that Brigadier Hicks had assumed temporary command of the division.

The first day of the operation had gone badly in every respect other than the landings, though this was not known to anyone outside the 1st Airborne Division. Back in England the second lift units were preparing to embark, and Captain Stewart Mawson – Medical Officer of 11th Parachute Battalion – had heard a rather positive, though ill-informed, briefing about the first lift and felt confident enough to tell his batman, Private A. T. Adams, that their part in the business would 'obviously be a piece of cake' (Stewart Mawson, 1981).

In reality, although Colonel Frost's 2nd Battalion, 'C' Company from Fitch's 3rd Battalion and much of 1st Parachute Brigade Headquarters, along with some gunners, engineers and others, had taken the northern end of the Arnhem road bridge, they had not been able to complete the task of securing the objective, and the battalions that had spent the latter part of the previous day trying to reach the bridge had been prevented from making their way to the target, suffering heavy casualties and a great deal of disruption. Many more men had become detached from their units than had actually been killed or wounded, but the effect was that the 1st and 3rd Parachute Battalions were now seriously weakened. Lieutenant Colonel Dobie's 1st Battalion had not actually halted during the night of 17–18 September. It had changed its angle of approach to avoid unnecessary contact with the enemy but had not been able to get any rest. The battalion had initially made some progress in the dark but was brought to a halt by German opposition at a railway

Paratroops waiting to embark for Arnhem. (Courtesy of Piers Gilliver)

crossing just outside Oosterbeek, and so around nightfall Dobie had chosen to head south in the hope of finding a way to reach Arnhem bridge without incurring the sort of casualties that would prevent his battalion from making a positive contribution to the defence of the objective. He led his battalion out of Oosterbeek to the south branch of the railway line that ran to a bridge over the Neder Rijn. Under the original plan, a company of 2nd Battalion would have secured this bridge and then pressed onward on the southern bank so that the road bridge could be attacked from both ends at once. This had not been achieved because on the preceding day the central segment of the railway bridge had been blown up just as the airborne troops set foot on the northern approach.

The railway line runs on a long and steep embankment that forms an effective barrier to the east of Oosterbeek. This proved too well guarded to be taken without paying a heavy price in casualties, so at about 0530 Dobie decided to move further to the south in search of an easier passage. In due course, the battalion – or rather the

Arnhem railway station.

elements of the battalion that had not become detached with 'R' company, such as the mortar platoon and the anti-tank guns – came to Oosterbeek Laag (lower) station, where they met up with men from 3rd Battalion who had become separated from the main body of their unit. The Germans had not deployed at the underpass where the road passed under the railway line but had taken up positions in houses a few hundred metres to the east of it, where they would have good fields of fire.

Despite his best efforts to avoid a major engagement, Dobie now had no choice but to try and fight his way into Arnhem since the river now prevented him from taking another detour to the south. The elements of 3rd Battalion that Dobie had taken under his command at the station were a welcome addition to his force and he was now able to call on the support of the divisional artillery. The Germans, though, were in good positions and only gave up territory at a measured pace, allowing each sub-unit to find new positions to the rear before the forward elements passed through. Progress was

The railway underpass on the route of 2nd Battalion, the Parachute Regiment.

painfully slow and casualties were heavy. By 1600 the battalion was still a long way from the bridge. A plan was formulated to load all the jeeps of the battalion with men and ammunition and attempt a dash through to the bridge, but the jeeps could not be found, or at least not in sufficient numbers to make the proposition viable. By the time it was getting dark, the battalion had run out of steam and was forced to take up positions a short distance short from the St Elisabeth Hospital, not far from where the remnants of 3rd Battalion had ended their day.

The situation was no better with the rest of 3rd Battalion. After a discussion with the brigade commander and the divisional commander, Colonel Fitch decided to lead the rest of the battalion south, away from his original route, and through Oosterbeek to the road that Frost's men had used the day before. They made good time until they reached the vicinity of the Rhine Pavilion, where the Rijnhotel stands today. As day broke, the battalion came under fire from isolated machine guns and snipers, which caused repeated delays and disrupted the column to such an extent that

The St Elisabeth Hospital.

'A' Company, the battalion's support elements and most of a troop of anti-tank guns ended up taking a different route to the balance of the battalion, leaving Colonel Fitch with just 'B' Company and a small party of Royal Engineers – not to mention the brigade and divisional commanders. In the meantime, Fitch had little choice other than to do what he could to concentrate the balance of his command. His leading platoon (No. 5, commanded by Lieutenant Cleminson) was ordered to wait for the rest of Fitch's force to catch up and, with luck, for the missing elements of the battalion to rejoin the column. In due course the rest of the battalion would encounter 1st Battalion as it too tried to force a path through to the bridge, but they were, effectively, lost to Colonel Fitch. Knowing that Fitch's battalion had come to a halt – in fact the leading platoon had been ordered to withdraw to the rest of the unit – the Germans were able to take some tentative action themselves. Snipers and machine guns in the brickworks on the far side of the river, and some infantry and one or two armoured vehicles on the northern side, were able to force Fitch's troops to take cover and keep them at bay for the rest of the morning. 1st Battalion was little more than half a mile away, but there was little prospect of achieving a union of the two units. Wireless communication was established, though, and it was decided that an attempt should be made to get ammunition to Fitch's men so that they could carry on with their move to the bridge. Accordingly, Lieutenant Leo Heaps, who had flown in with 1st Battalion and was one of the many Canadian officers in the division, took two Bren Carriers piled high with ammunition and a party of infantry under Lieutenant Burwash, commander of 3rd Battalion's Pioneer Platoon, and made contact with Fitch in the early afternoon. The attack was renewed, but to no great purpose; the Germans had deployed more than enough troops in the area to prevent Fitch's men from getting to the bridge.

2nd Battalion had done what it could to strengthen its positions through the night of 17 September, and to get what rest it could, hopeful that XXX Corps would arrive by the end of the day. Two attempts had been made to rush the far end of the bridge during the night. Neither were successful, but this was probably not a great worry to Colonel Frost, who – not unreasonably – thought that the rest of 1st Brigade would join his battalion before too long and that they would provide the necessary strength to force a crossing, or that XXX Corps, when it arrived, would drive the enemy from the far end of the bridge. At daybreak a convoy of German trucks loaded with infantry came into sight and was roughly handled, to be followed soon after by an attack consisting of more than twenty vehicles – armoured cars, half-tracks and trucks – of 9th SS Panzer Division's reconnaissance battalion. The leading vehicles managed to avoid a chain of mines set across the road, drove straight through the battalion's positions and on into Arnhem, but the rest fell victim to Frost's PIATs, Gammon bombs and anti-tank guns. From an attic in Frost's tiny perimeter, Major Mumford was able to call in strikes from the guns of 1st Airlanding Light Regiment and a third attack was swiftly broken up. For a short while Frost's signallers managed to make contact with XXX Corps. It was still a long way from the objective, but the operation was only in its early stages and there seemed to be no reason to doubt that the corps would arrive before too long. A little after that, the battalion's 'B' company, which the previous day had been detached to take the pontoon bridge, managed to rejoin the unit, providing a welcome reinforcement to Frost's command, bringing it up to a strength of about 700 men. In the early part of the day the defenders at the bridge had been able to hear a good deal of firing from the vicinity of the St Elisabeth Hospital to the west, but Frost had no real knowledge of the situation there, only that the sound of firing did not seem to be coming any closer.

The wider picture was not terribly encouraging. When he took command of the division, Brigadier Hicks had found himself in a difficult position. He had little information about what was happening in Arnhem – though obviously the plan was not going well – and his options were limited. His own brigade had discharged its tasks effectively, but he could be confident that the Germans would be doing whatever they could to disrupt his battalions and might attack in strength at any moment. Thus far, the Airlanding Brigade units had been able to deal with enemy activity, but at some point there would undoubtedly be a properly co-ordinated effort to dislodge them. The second lift was due to arrive and it was of paramount importance that its drops and landings should be carried out with as little interference from the enemy as possible. Equally, it was all too clear that the advance into Arnhem had been stopped in its tracks. The best that could be said was that half of the most significant objective had been secured and that its value was being denied to the enemy. But the force at the bridge was not that large and would be vulnerable to armoured attacks – Frost's command could be shelled into oblivion were the Germans to prevent reinforcements from passing through the town. If the bridge were not secured, the entire operation would have been a waste of effort. Unless the bridge could be held, the arrival of 4th Brigade would be an irrelevance at best. Hicks had no real reserve to commit to the fight; all the infantry units already had tasks that could not be abandoned. The King's Own Scottish Borderers and the Border Regiment were, in any case, a long way from the town; it would take them several hours to withdraw from their current positions, concentrate, march to Arnhem and deploy for battle. The only possible course of action was to send Colonel McCardle's South Staffordshires into the Arnhem battle in the hope that they would tip the balance of the struggle in favour of the airborne troops. Hicks assigned a party from the GliderPilot Regiment and elements of the Reconnaissance Squadron to take responsibility for the relevant landing area, and the Staffordshires duly moved off toward the town at 1000 according to the Brigade Headquarters diary.

Preparations for the second lift were carried out on schedule. The Independent Company platoons had set off at first light to establish their equipment for the arrival of the second lift. This would prove to be a more difficult process than on the previous day. Each of the platoons had to lay out its identification panels and smoke, and also erect its Eureka equipment in the face of some degree of enemy opposition. The supply drop at LZ 'L' was due at 1000 but delayed by poor weather conditions, and No. 1 Platoon came under attack from a group of German fighter aircraft at around 1200. It was here that the first news was received of the wider picture of the operation – that one end of the main target had been taken by 2nd Battalion, but that the balance of 1st Brigade was struggling to make progress through the town to reinforce it and take the other end of the bridge.

Number 1 platoon would have to wait until 1530 before the transport aircraft carrying the second lift arrived, as would No. 2 Platoon at 'X' and No. 3 Platoon at 'Y'. In each case the arrival of the convoys was met by a considerable weight of enemy fire, but the tasks were carried out effectively and although the second

Attracting the attention of supply-drop pilots.

lift incurred rather higher losses than the first, it was a reasonably effective landing. However, the delay of several hours had afforded the Germans more time to analyse the situation and deploy reinforcements to the best effect.

Sergeant Keith Banwell of the 10th Battalion's stick had been on the verge of jumping when a burst of machine gun fire tore along the side of its Dakota, killing six of the occupants and leaving the remainder to clamber over the corpses to exit the aircraft before it crashed into the woodland surrounding the drop zone. Banwell would spend the next two days on the heath before he was able to make his way into what was, by then, the divisional perimeter.

Despite the delay and a greater degree of opposition, the drops and landings were remarkably successful, even though the air was not as still as it had been the previous day. Losses from all the units were much higher than during the first lift, but this is a little misleading. Some units were reduced by more than 100 men, but the initial landings and drops had been extremely good; better in fact than might normally be expected in an exercise where there was no enemy action at all. Each of the 1st Parachute Brigade battalions had been able to gather well over 90 per cent of their men within a short space of time. The average initial shortfall when the second-lift troops gathered at the unit rendezvous points would seem to have amounted to about 20 per cent – well within the parameters of what might be expected in any airborne operation. Moreover, unit commanders would have expected that some of the shortfall would be recovered in the course of the operation. Some of the men who had landed too far from the DZ to join their units by the time they moved off to their objectives would catch up, and some men would have been in aircraft that had had to abort their flight and would, in theory, return to their airfields and be flown in with the lift scheduled for Tuesday 19 September. Naturally, there were several injuries of the sort that might be expected from parachute jumping. The chaplain of 10th Battalion, Captain Bowers, broke his ankle on landing, and another chaplain, Captain Menzies of 156th Battalion, was caught in the breeze as he landed and dragged for some distance before he could get his parachute under control, and then had to cut himself free from his harness before he could get on with his duties.

Inevitably, a number of sticks were dropped prematurely or their aircraft overshot the LZ and dropped the men well beyond the battle area. Two sticks of 133 Field Ambulance found themselves not far from Otterlo, about 10km to the north-west of Arnhem. The men – including surgeon Major Brian Courtney – and their equipment would both be sadly missed over the next eight days. If the troop landings and drops were reasonably successful, the same could not

Waiting for the next attack.

be said of the supply drop. All but two of the thirty-three Stirling bombers that were assigned to the task were able to deliver their loads to LZ 'L' just north of the railway line, but the LZ had not been secured. Some supplies were lost from the two Stirlings that did not reach the LZ, but more than 700 supply canisters and cane panniers out of approximately 800 were found. Only about 15 per cent of the stores, though, were recovered. The basic nine-battalion structure of the division – two parachute and one airlanding brigade, the anti-tank gun batteries, the airlanding artillery regiment, the Royal Engineers, Royal Army Medical Corps (RAMC) and Royal Army Service Corps (RASC) – was present and had arrived in good shape, but there was already potential for a serious shortage of supplies of all kinds. The RASC detachment had made particularly good time. Despite considerable mortar and small arms fire on its LZ, little more than an hour after landing at Oosterbeek it had unloaded its gliders and moved to the middle of the divisional area. Lieutenant Colonel Packe – the Commander, Royal Army Service Corps (CRASC) – had established his headquarters and the Divisional Maintenance Area (DMA) close to the Hartenstein Hotel, and made arrangements for collecting and stacking the supplies, which – according to the plan – would be delivered every day. The divisional area was quite extensive by this time and the RASC Headquarters was able to get on with its tasks without interruption for the rest of the day, other than the customary stand-to at dusk.

When the day's landings had been completed, the platoons of the Independent Company made their rendezvous at Reijers Camp at 1800, and an hour later they moved off to take up a position around a large house called 'St Paulastichting', near Oosterbeek Hoog station. This area would become very familiar over the next few days.

While the Independent Company set about its tasks, men in the second lift were making their way to the battle. Harry Faulkner-Brown, like Urquhart the previous day, noticed the many rescue craft in the Channel. He and his comrades experienced some flak, but few of the transports were hit. He was the first man in his stick and had a struggle to get two folding bicycles out of the Dakota before being able to jump. His stick landed safely as did most of his squadron, but his superior, Major Aeneas Perkins, had dislocated his shoulder and was expected to be out of the battle for some days. The Acting Commanding Officer, Captain Thomas Beaumont, sent a party to look for men and canisters, most of which had been scattered about the heath, and the majority of the squadron and its equipment were then gathered in without too much difficulty. Faulkner-Brown was informed that the previous day's advance had been held up by stronger resistance than had been anticipated and that they were now to advance along the route of the railway instead of taking the main road to Arnhem. Accordingly, they moved off to a position near the railway line and set about making defensive measures and settling in for the night. Clearly, the arrival of the second lift was not going to be enough to restore the timetable that Urquhart had put in place for the achievement of the D+1 objectives, but the squadron was in good heart and confident that progress would be made the following day.

In point of fact, the situation had not really improved with the arrival of the second lift. Hicks had done what he could to force the pace of the advance into Arnhem by sending the South Staffordshires to support the attack, but little was being gained. According to the South Staffordshires' diary, the battalion set off at 1030 having received its orders at 0900 – an indication that the decision to redeploy the battalion from its planned role had already been made before Hicks formally assumed command of the division (Battalion Diary, Pegasus Archive). The move began well, but within a short space of time it had run into serious resistance to the north of Oosterbeek, which kept the men occupied for some considerable time and they were forced to detour to the south. It was not until daylight was fading that the force was able to join what remained of 1st and 3rd Parachute Battalions a little over 1km from the bridge.

There was a limit to what the South Staffordshires might achieve because they were not a full battalion; more than half of their combat strength had been left behind in England due to the shortage of gliders and towing aircraft and were not due to arrive until the second lift in mid-morning. Two companies ('A' and 'C'), half of the battalion's Vickers guns and anti-tank guns and the mortar platoon were still en route, and, in addition to the casualties incurred in action, one platoon of 'B' Company and the company headquarters glider had failed to arrive in the first lift. In practice, the battalion had only about one-third of its men as it moved off towards the town. As soon as the rest of the battalion arrived with the second lift they were to be sent on toward Arnhem. One company would catch up with its comrades at midnight on 18 September, but the balance of the unit would not arrive until dawn on the following day.

Hicks was well aware that the South Staffordshires – even at full strength – were unlikely to turn the situation around and had decided that one of Hackett's battalions should be directed to advance into Arnhem to support the attack as quickly as possible. The northern, 'Leopard' route had not been secured during the first day's operations and 11th Battalion's rendezvous was the most convenient, so Hicks decided that the battalion should be assigned to the task. There was no means of conveying this change of plan to Brigadier Hackett since he and his men were already in the air when the decision was made. Understandably, Hackett was less than impressed that a decision had been made in his absence but accepted that the attack had to be reinforced and that 11th Battalion was best placed for the task.

The battalion was able to concentrate quickly after landing and made excellent time until it came to the vicinity of the divisional headquarters, which had moved to the Hartenstein Hotel and was operational by 1700. Here the battalion was kept waiting for some considerable time – the commander of 'A' company, Major David Gilchrist, would later describe this period as 'sitting on our backsides for several hours' (Pegasus Archive). This may have been something of an exaggeration, but clearly there was a lengthy delay at a critical juncture, and by the time both 11th Battalion and the South Staffordshires made their way into the town as far as the streets to the west of the St Elisabeth Hospital it was midnight. Both of these battalions were reasonably fresh. They had sustained few casualties and had not expended a great deal of ammunition. When added to the remnants of 1st and 3rd Battalions – whose combined strength was now only 150, all ranks, according to reports to Divisional Headquarters – they constituted a substantial force. But there was no mechanism to ensure that their efforts could be properly co-ordinated since the most appropriate headquarters unit – 1st Parachute Brigade Headquarters – was now surrounded at the objective, and in any case both the brigade commander and the divisional commander – though not far away – were quite unable to influence the battle. The previous afternoon, Urquhart and Lathbury had decided to press on to the bridge only to find themselves cut off by German troops and forced to take shelter. Lathbury, wounded in the back, was unable to move, and it soon became clear that they could not stay where they were. German troops were starting to search the area and Lathbury had been left in the care of a Dutch family while Urquhart and two other officers (Lieutenant Cleminson and Captain Taylor) sought an alternative haven. They found it at the home of the Derksen family at No. 14 Zwarteweg. Entering by the kitchen door, they were quickly directed upstairs to a bedroom. Captain Taylor found a tiny attic above a room that would give them a view of the street below, and the three men duly climbed in, pulling the ladder up behind them, and settled in to await an opportunity to rejoin the division once the Germans had moved on. They would have a long wait; Urquhart would not be able to rejoin his headquarters until early on the morning of 19 September, having been out of the battle for a day and a half.

Brigadier Lathbury.

Logbook of navigator R.S. Taylor of 238 Squadron RAF, flying from South Blakehill Farm.

While Urquhart and his companions fretted in an Arnhem attic, there was some activity in the Airlanding Brigade area. A store of twenty-one new 105mm guns was found and duly destroyed by a platoon of 9th Field Company at about 1500, and at 1700 the Brigade Main Dressing Station started a move toward Arnhem, leaving the factory that it had requisitioned in Wolfheze. The move was not completed, though, until the following day due to the need to move the wounded men with great care. As the day came to a close, the brigade – less the South Staffordshires – relocated to the east and took up positions around the northern and western aspects of Oosterbeek. The King's Own Scottish Borderers established themselves to the north of the railway around Johanna Hoeve Farm, and the Border Regiment formed a series of positions running from Heveadorp to the Brigade Headquarters and elements of the Glider Pilot Regiment at Bilderberg.

Whatever hard words had passed between Hicks and Hackett over the matter of detaching one of the latter's battalions, the two men

Johanna Hoeve Farm.

had now come to terms with the situation. Hicks had decided that the balance of 4th Brigade should now advance to Arnhem parallel to and north of the railway, with 156th Battalion taking the lead. By dusk it had become necessary to order 156th to halt and regroup before carrying on down the railway line at first light. 11th Battalion, still at the drop zone, was ordered to remain there until 0330, when it was to follow the rest of the brigade. Late that night Hackett went to Divisional Headquarters to meet Brigadier Hicks and they agreed that 4th Brigade's programme for the next day would be to press on along the northern edge of Oosterbeek and occupy an area of high ground, known as Koepel, on the south side of the 'Leopard' route and within striking distance of the supply DZ 'V'. As a consequence, the two remaining battalions and the other elements of 4th Brigade would spend the night strung out in a long line that stretched almost all the way to Wolfheze, which would hamper their ability to concentrate forces in the morning.

5

D+2: TUESDAY 19 SEPTEMBER

Hackett's Brigade attempted to renew its advance at 0400 but found the path into Arnhem blocked by a strong German defence, including many armoured vehicles, which would be the story of the day for much of the division. The four battalions (1st, 3rd, 11th Parachute Battalions and the South Staffordshires), which were already in the town and endeavouring to reach Frost's command, were, by this time, disrupted and scattered and had already suffered heavy casualties. The absence of a generally understood plan for these units – indeed, the absence of any real co-ordinated plan at all above battalion level – led to a great deal of confusion, made all the worse because of high casualties among the officers and senior NCOs. Some men responded to the challenge by taking on duties that were far removed from their normal responsibilities. At one point the chaplain of 1st Battalion, Captain Watkins, led a patrol through the streets in search of men who had become detached from their units and was able to bring back a party of 11th Battalion men who had become isolated in houses along the Utrechtseweg. He had to abandon further efforts, though, in the face of heavy fire. Laudable as such actions were, they were no substitute for the sort of proper command and control structure that would have been imposed by an active brigade headquarters. Consequently, the actions of the units were not as effective as they might have been. It is not at all clear, however, that even the best of plans or most proactive leadership would really have made a significant difference. The German forces that barred the way to Arnhem bridge were simply too powerful and could, if necessary, have been reinforced by troops drawn from the fighting to the north-west without seriously compromising the defence that was holding up 4th Brigade.

The arrival of the second lift had rendered the defence of 4th Brigade's DZ unnecessary, and the failure of the advance to the north of Arnhem meant that the brigade was still in the vicinity of the railway line stretching from Oosterbeek to Wolfheze. Establishing a safe cordon around the proposed supply zone and the LZ for the glider element of the Polish Brigade was imperative for the division to collect the ammunition and food necessary to continue the fight and to ensure that the mortars, transport and anti-tank guns of the Poles would not be overrun as they landed.

With one of his battalions detached to support the battle in the town, and in the face of opposition that had prevented his men from acquiring their objectives during the previous day, Hackett obviously would not have the manpower to fight for and retain the LZs without significant additional resources – a principle that had been agreed with Hicks while he had temporary command of the division. At 0800, the King's Own Scottish Borderers came under the command of 4th Brigade to take the place of the battalion that had been sent to reinforce the units in Arnhem. This was certainly the most practical approach to the situation since the Borderers were closer to 4th Brigade than any of the other infantry assets, although it also compromised the brigade plan of Hicks' own command since he had already deployed the South Staffordshires to Arnhem. The Airlanding Brigade would now have to fulfil its obligations with only one battalion – the Border Regiment – and the various brigade assets and elements of the Glider Pilot Regiment. There was one brighter development: at 0900 Hicks was able to resume his role as a brigade commander, following the return of General Urquhart.

By this time a number of problems had arisen. Reports to divisional headquarters from elements of the Reconnaissance Squadron and from Royal Artillery forward observation posts had brought news of an enemy concentration to the north of LZ 'L', where the gliders of the Polish Brigade were due to arrive later in the day, with further reports of extensive German movements near Renkum and in the Doorwerth woods. If the Germans continued to move east along the river bank, the Airborne Division could soon be surrounded.

The planned supply drop area to the east of the Lichtenbeek woods had not been secured, LZ 'L' was under threat and the only realistic alternative LZ or DZ would be the polder (an area of reclaimed land) to the south of Oosterbeek Laag station. However, that area had already been ruled out for gliders because of the softness of the ground and it would also be in full view of German observers on the south bank of the Neder Rijn. Even if the RAF were prepared to accept the polder area as an alternative – and there was no guarantee that it would – the state of communications was such that it was less than likely that the arrangements could be made in time for the Tuesday drop. Moreover, even if such arrangements could be made, the Germans were quite capable of reading maps – if they had occupied all the practical landing areas as outlined in the British airlift plan in their possession since Sunday, they would be able to deduce that the zone bounded by Oosterbeek church, the station and the Neder Rijn was the only alternative – and it would not take a strategic genius to deploy all the anti-aircraft assets in the vicinity to take advantage of the situation.

A report in the divisional diary at 1015 (Pegasus Archive) saying that the tanks of XXX Corps had reached Grave can hardly have inspired confidence either. The ground forces, already well overdue, had only covered half of their planned advance. An hour later, the

Divisional Headquarters received news that the South Staffordshires had fought their way into the town but sustained many casualties and were now under heavy artillery and mortar fire. Clearly, they were not going to make rapid progress towards the bridge. Unable to move forwards, and very possibly with a growing enemy presence to their rear, the South Staffordshires had little choice but to adopt a defensive posture and hope that they would be relieved by another thrust into the town. Their Medical Officer (MO), Captain Brownscombe, and the chaplain – Captain Buchanan – set up the Regimental Aid Post in the cellars of the Arnhem municipal museum (described in some accounts as 'the monastery') on the Utrechtseweg, less than quarter of a mile from the St Elisabeth Hospital. Like his fellow chaplain Captain Watkins, Buchanan found himself drawn into the battle and discharging command duties that were well outside the bounds of his calling. Among other things, he ordered a platoon from the battalion's 'A' Company to take up a position to protect the museum. It was hardly his job to make tactical decisions or issue combat orders, but there were now few officers that had not been killed or wounded and somebody had to take charge.

If there was no good news from Arnhem, there was an equal dearth of it from elsewhere. At 0945, Brigadier Hackett informed Divisional Headquarters that the King's Own Scottish Borderers – still under his command at this point – had made an attack during the night toward Lichtenbeek but had been unable to make progress, retiring to Johanna Hoeve Farm to avoid being caught in the open when day broke. Strangely, though, Hackett made no mention of this incident in the Brigade Headquarters diary, which he compiled after the battle.

Abandoning any attempt to secure the supply drop zone and the LZ for the Polish support elements was not an option, and Hackett pressed on with the fight, issuing orders accordingly. His two parachute battalions were to mount attacks – 156th to secure Koepel and 10th to move through the woods to the north of Johanna Hoeve Farm. Once there, they would secure the main road from Amsterdam and thereby protect the flank of 156th Battalion and prevent the enemy from approaching the supply drop zone from the north-west.

At 0900, Hackett visited 156th at Johanna Hoeve and found that a company-level attack to the east was going well, with few casualties. The plan was to clear the Lichtenbeek area to the east of Johanna Hoeve and then launch an attack to take Koepel. The King's Own Scottish Borderers were deployed on the left of the brigade area to ensure the safe arrival of the glider-borne elements of 1st Polish Independent Parachute Brigade on LZ 'L'.

Before long, 10th Battalion ran into a strong German force on the very position on the 'Leopard' route to which they had been directed earlier in the day and received permission for what Brigadier Hackett described as a 'bolder west flanking movement', presumably along the wooded eastern edge of LZ 'L'. When Hackett returned to his Brigade Headquarters at 1030, he learned that Urquhart was now back in command and would like to meet him if he could get away, or, failing that, Urquhart would come to him.. Hackett now felt the situation was 'looking tidier' than had been the case when he had arrived, although it was still far from promising. By midday, 10th Battalion occupied roughly the position that Hackett had intended but was quite heavily engaged from the north and east, though not yet from the main road to the west, which had been considered the most likely avenue for an enemy attack. Meanwhile, 156th Battalion had launched two company-strength attacks to take Lichtenbeek, both of which had come to nothing, with heavy casualties. As Hackett put it, the battalion had, for the time being, 'shot its bolt'.

Hackett had been informed that elements of the Airlanding Brigade would make a new attack to secure the crossing at the Oosterbeek railway halt at 1500, and he gave instructions that 156th should provide whatever support it could muster. Urquhart visited shortly after 1400 and told Hackett something about his absence in Arnhem but could give little information about the condition of 11th Battalion. Reports from division at around the time that Airlanding Brigade was scheduled to make its attack to seize the Oosterbeek Halt crossing indicated that there had either been or might shortly be a successful enemy attack in the area to the south of the railway.

Hackett had discussed the difficult nature of his position with Urquhart during the general's visit, pointing out that the railway embankment was too great an obstacle for his transport and that without possession of the Oosterbeek crossing his brigade might easily be split in two. Hackett's proposal was that he should bring all of his units south of the railway and reorient his brigade axis to the Utrecht road instead of along the Amsterdam–Arnhem highway. Urquhart was amenable to this, convinced that the supply drop area could not now be captured, and arranged for signals to be sent to Britain to have both the supply drop zone and the Polish landing zones changed.

In the event, the signals did not reach their destination. Given the poor state of communications generally it seems rather optimistic for Urquhart to have assumed that they had, and more so to have acted on that assumption when he received no acknowledgement of his request.

Urquhart also instructed Hackett to disengage, cross the railway, take up positions to the east of Oosterbeek and, if possible, make contact with 11th Battalion. If this move was to be accomplished without losing his transport and anti-tank guns, Hackett would have to order 10th Battalion to disengage and move 3km west to occupy the crossing at Wolfheze, which had not, as far as he knew, been occupied by the enemy.

Hackett's brigade diary is not entirely clear about the order of events. He relates that reports from 10th Battalion had become both confused and intermittent and that 'a difficult position was developing for them'. He wrote that he had learned subsequently that the enemy had occupied the position at which the battalion was to rendezvous after disengagement, which naturally led to some confusion and disorganisation. He had also learned that the order to disengage had already been given, with 1515 as the 'possible time', though the divisional diary is clear that the brigade started to implement the plan at 1500. At first glance, the plan was a curious one given that it would almost inevitably result in the eastern flank of the Polish landing being exposed to enemy fire – and since Urquhart had received no response to his signal about changing the Polish and supply landing zones it was unrealistic to take it for granted that any action had been taken in that regard. Hackett describes 10th Battalion as passing across the LZ in 'very fair order' as the Polish gliders arrived. In fact the battalion had retired more than a kilometre in an hour at most. Urquhart had been able to see the rear two battalions a few hundred metres away across the fields when he had visited Hackett's Headquarters about 2 hours earlier and noted that both were thinly stretched.

In the meantime, Hackett had become aware that the Border Regiment had come under attack from a strong German force with powerful armour and artillery support around Renkum and Heelsum, just a few kilometres to the south-west. The Border Regiment had an enormous front to hold – several kilometres in rolling countryside that might afford the enemy more than one covered route into the heart of the divisional area. There was certainly potential for the enemy to keep the Border Regiment companies heavily engaged and pass a column through as far as the railway line and possibly cut Hackett's brigade off completely from the divisional area. For all practical purposes, every infantry unit in the vicinity had reached the end of its respective tether for the time being. Both 10th and 156th Battalions had mounted several attacks in the space of 24 hours and had suffered considerable casualties, as had the King's Own Scottish Borderers, who had been in action the previous day as well. A withdrawal across the railway line would have some potential to ease the situation of 4th Brigade. It might prove possible to give the brigade a defensible northern boundary since the embankment was so steep and because it might be practical to cover the line itself with well-sited machine guns. Additionally, the embankment would be a serious challenge for enemy vehicles, and therefore the available anti-tank guns could be positioned to cover the crossing points. It would also be an admission that any chance of securing the supply drop zone was no longer viable and that there was no real hope of mounting a fresh attack into Arnhem. Every unit in the division was already engaged or, at the very least, in a position from which it could not be withdrawn without providing a new opportunity for a German attack into the divisional area.

Hackett had been dealt an unplayable hand and done the best he could with it. Throughout the day, he had consistently displayed remarkable gallantry and was undoubtedly an inspiration to his men. John Waddy (commander of 156th Battalion's 'B' Company) described one incident that occurred as 4th Brigade was fighting in the Wolfheze woods to the north of Oosterbeek after the withdrawal across the Polish landing zone:

> In a clearing in the woods I saw 3 jeeps, and on the trailer of one a wounded man lay motionless. Germans were darting through the woods; the squat barrel of an SP gun appeared, it fired and hit one of the jeeps, which burst into flames. A driver ran from it shouting that it was loaded with ammunition. We all waited in horror for the explosion: then out of the trees a short spare figure ran to the burning vehicle – it was the brigadier! Springing into the driver's seat of the jeep with the wounded man he gunned the engine into life, and the jeep and trailer roared across the clearing.
>
> (John Patrick O'Reilly, 2009)

The delay of the third lift had made 4th Brigade's task virtually impossible and at the same time had afforded the Germans an opportunity to improve their own situation. They had brought a large number of anti-aircraft assets to the Arnhem area throughout 18 September and, thanks to the map they had of the scheduled landing and drop zones, were able to deploy them with considerable effect, though in practice the LZ and DZ for the third lift were fairly obvious. Consequently, the lift of the Polish glider element and the supply lift scheduled on 19 September suffered far more heavily from German anti-aircraft fire than the previous two landings. Losses might well have been even heavier had it not been for the cancellation of the parachute element of the Polish brigade, which would otherwise have been dropped more than a kilometre to the south of the Arnhem bridge. It is arguably possible that if the drop had gone ahead, the Poles could have attacked and captured the southern end of the bridge, and relieved Frost's troops. Had that happened, it is not inconceivable that the bridge might still have been held when XXX Corps arrived, or even that the knowledge that the main objective was in Allied hands would have spurred Horrocks to force the pace of his advance. More realistically, there is every chance that the Poles would have landed on a drop zone held by the enemy and been cut to pieces. With their anti-tank gun, mortar and machine gun platoons landing several kilometres away on the far side of the river, the Poles would have been vulnerable to even the lightest of German armour. Tanks, self-propelled guns and flak vehicles could have simply positioned themselves out of the range of PIATs and doused the area with fire. Many of the British defenders in Oosterbeek and Arnhem had been able to take cover in buildings or had had the opportunity to dig themselves into the light soil before the Germans could mount major attacks, but the Poles were to drop into open country. The brigade was certainly a powerful force, but it would be incredibly vulnerable in the air and during the actual landing process, and it would also have been virtually impossible for the units to concentrate effectively while under fire. There was a good chance that the Poles would have been virtually, if not entirely, surrounded.

German anti-aircraft gun in a ground-support role.

After a delay for poor weather, the Polish gliderelement arrived on
LZ 'L' at 1630. Hackett's description of the events of the afternoon
rather suggests that the Poles reacted poorly; that there was some
firing at the LZ, but little of it and most of it very high. His report
includes an implication that the Poles opened fire on the retreating
4th Brigade troops indiscriminately as soon as they left their gliders.
There has to be a suspicion that Hackett was less than accurate in
his assessment of the situation. His two parachute battalions may not
have been retreating in quite as controlled a manner as he suggests,
though it would seem that the Germans, under the command of the
same officer – Krafft – who had done so much to stall the advance
to Arnhem on 17 September, did not pursue their attack with as

much vigour as they might have done. This is hardly surprising given the fact that they, like the airborne troops, had seen a great deal of fighting over the previous two days. Moreover, the German plan was essentially a matter of containing the airborne troops so that they could be shelled into surrender or starved out. Either way, there was no pressing need for the Germans to force an immediate conclusion to the battle; to do so would incur unnecessary casualties in an action that to all intents and purposes had already been won.

The Divisional Headquarters diary recorded the landing in a rather different light, stating that the Polish force was 'very heavily opposed from ground and air and suffered severe casualties' (Pegasus Archive). It has been suggested that the Poles failed to identify troops around their LZ as British and that there were language difficulties. This may have been the case, but it is perhaps more relavent to consider the issue of visibility. The Poles certainly landed in an area that was under fire from the north and east. They were aware of troops on the LZ itself but also that there were more approaching the zone from the surrounding woods. It would have been extremely difficult to identify the nationality of men in woodland – especially men in camouflage smocks – at anything beyond very close range, and since there were British soldiers retiring across the LZ it would be a reasonable conclusion that that they were being pursued by the troops in the woods.

Despite the fiasco on the LZ, a significant proportion of the Poles who had managed to land safely were able to get off the LZ. No aspect of the day's endeavours, though, was going well. Around dusk, 4th Brigade reported that it had been unable to disengage, that it had moved south of the railway and met 'further opposition there, which would prevent movement during darkness'. None of these factors should have come as a surprise. The brigade was facing competent and experienced troops under competent commanders. The Germans might not be in a hurry to force the pace of the battle to achieve an immediate outcome, but equally they were most unlikely to allow the enemy to break off contact on their own terms. To do so would simply give them an opportunity to reorganise, acquire supplies and select good positions to continue the fight at daybreak. In fact, a report to Divisional Headquarters stated that a German prisoner of war had claimed that there would be an attack in some strength – two companies and some armoured vehicles – at 0300. An attack on such a scale would not have been an attempt to destroy what remained of 4th Brigade, but one simply to ensure as much disruption as possible and prevent the tired British troops from getting any sleep. Even if the attack had only been pressed for a few minutes, it might well have resulted in the whole body of airborne troops having to stand-to for some time after the Germans had withdrawn. Additionally, given the nature of forest fighting, the British would probably have expended a great deal of ammunition, which by now was in short supply in the brigade area. The attack failed to materialise, though enemy troops and vehicles were heard nearby.

Searching a German prisoner of war.

Fortunately, the brigade's engineers – 4th Parachute Squadron – had found a tunnel through the railway embankment. It was quickly discovered that by letting a quantity of air out of the tyres of the jeeps they could pass through to the other side and thereby avoid driving the extra kilometres to Wolfheze. This was just as well, since 10th Battalion had found that the Wolfheze crossing has occupied by the enemy and they had to clear their route, but some of the transport had to be abandoned and efforts to recover it the next day were not successful. By the end of the day, 4th Brigade had managed to take positions south of the embankment, with 10th Battalion close to Wolfheze and 156th to the left. However, they had a total force of only about 500 men.

It had been a long day for the infantry battalions of 4th Brigade, and it had really been no better for the other units. Harry Faulkner-Brown and his comrades had woken around dawn and set off along the track running parallel to the railway line as far as the level

Germans using a captured jeep to transport wounded prisoners of war.

crossing at Wolfheze, where they saw a string of railway flatcars carrying anti-aircraft guns that had been destroyed on 17 September. Shortly thereafter, Faulkner-Brown and his comrades were reunited with the glider element of squadron with their jeeps and trailers full of engineering stores and then joined by Major Perkins, whose dislocated shoulder had been reset by a doctor at 133 Parachute Field Ambulance.

For a brief period the engineers thought that three or four German fighters were attacking them, but in fact they were firing at 156th Battalion some distance down the road. Thereafter the engineers continued the march eastward, finding a farm cart that they loaded with mines and other stores and which three men could easily handle in the absence of a horse. They had travelled only about a kilometre from Wolfheze when they were ordered to halt and take up a defensive position. In due course they upped sticks again and marched on as far as LZ 'L' and moved in beside a party from the Glider Pilot Regiment, where the jeeps and guns of the Poles were scheduled to arrive later in the day, but 10th Battalion was engaged against strong enemy forces that had been deployed on the north boundary. Major Perkins was summoned to a Brigade 'O' group and returned to inform the squadron that it was to take on an infantry role and guard against any enemy interference from the direction of Wolfheze, while 10th Battalion moved to secure defensive positions on the main road to the north of LZ 'L'. The arrival of the Poles and their departure from the LZ was followed by a fleet of 160 aircraft delivering stores to the prearranged supply DZ. Since the site was in German hands very little materiel was recovered and many aircraft were lost, including the Dakota of Flight Lieutenant David Lord who sacrificed his life to drop all his supplies and was awarded a posthumous Victoria Cross. It was at a Squadron 'O' group soon after that Major Perkins gave his men the news that 156th and 10th Battalions were going to disengage and retire across the embankment. For some hours the squadron was engaged in getting the jeeps through the culvert under the embankment. During that period, Major Perkins was informed that the Wolfheze crossing had been recovered from the enemy and he promptly ordered that all Bren Carriers, Morris Tractors and 17-pounder anti-tank guns should go there as quickly as possible.

With the squadron's task completed, the major was able to lead most of the force into the divisional area, where the Commander Royal Engineers (CRE), Lieutenant Colonel Myers, sent them to set up in a large four-storey house named 'Sonnenberg'. Faulkner-Brown had stayed behind with a party of sappers, watching the Germans pressing hard on the retreat of the rearmost elements of 4th Brigade, when he was blown off his feet by a large explosion. He was dazed but not wounded. It seems that a Corporal Berry of the King's Own Scottish Borderers had spotted a party of Germans about to seize the cart that the squadron had 'liberated' earlier and packed with mines and other stores. Berry fired a long burst from a

The culvert under the Oosterbeek–Wolfheze railway line.

Bren gun into the cart and detonated the cargo – something in the region of 50kg of explosives.

Still suffering from a degree of shock, Faulkner-Brown made his way into the divisional area and was directed to the Hartenstein Hotel. For a while he stood on the lawn at the hotel trying to gather any stray engineers and then he was called into Hartenstein and ordered to go to Ommershof – a substantial Victorian house on the northern aspect of the perimeter – where he and his party of sappers would act in an infantry role under the command of Major Wilson of the Independent Company. His party amounted to about twenty men, the rest of the squadron having gone to 'Sonnenberg', nearly a kilometre to the south. Faulkner-Brown led the group to Ommershof along Oranjeweg and got there about 1700. A road – Graaf von Rechterenweg – ran east to west across his front and Faulkner-Brown's party was to hold a stretch of about 100m, with the Independent Company to his right and, further right, the King's Own Scottish Borderers, who were digging in around the Dreyeroord Hotel – better known to the troops who served there as the 'White House'. Initially, the Independent Company was also responsible for holding the line south, down Oranjeweg, but were soon replaced by a party of sixty glider pilots, some more sappers and a Polish anti-tank gun that had survived the landing. In total, the engineers consisted of less than seventy men, including four officers.

By nightfall Faulkner-Brown and his trench-mate, Lance Corporal Dai Morris, had deepened their slit trench and lined it with a piece of parachute material and willow branches to help prevent the sandy soil from damaging their weapons. Some time after dark, Faulkner-Brown was ordered to investigate some nearby movement in the woods across the road only to discover it was a parachute caught in the trees being lit up by a burning house – a nerve-wracking experience, particularly for a man whose day had been so long and stressful.

Their neighbours for the night, the Independent Company, had spent the day divided. Two platoons had been trying to carry

The rear of the Dreyeroord Hotel – known as the 'White House'.

out their pathfinder duties at the DZ and LZ on the far side of the railway, while the other platoon and the company headquarters improved the position at the 'St Paulastichting' house. One of the two platoons that had gone to the DZ and LZ rejoined its comrades in the late afternoon, the other platoon some time after dusk, although the whole company was soon to move on to a new location. With increasing German activity around 'St Paulastichting', Major Wilson decided to move his command to an area around a different large house – 'Ommershof' – to ensure better fields of fire and to take advantage of mesh fences around other houses in the vicinity, which would impede any future infantry attack. The Independent Company had now completed the last of its specialist tasks. According to the original plan, it should now have been preparing to move to the south of the Neder Rijn to set up its equipment on DZ 'K' for the main drop of 1st Polish Independent Parachute Brigade. Clearly this was not going to be possible since the southern end of the Arnhem road bridge was in enemy hands. From this point on the role of the Independent Company would be to contribute to the defence of the increasingly hard-pressed perimeter at Oosterbeek.

The general picture at the close of the day was not a cheerful one. Fourth Brigade had been badly beaten up in a day of fierce combat to the north and was not out of the woods, either literally or figuratively, since it had yet to make secure contact with the divisional area and was still engaged with the enemy among the trees and clearings along the south of the railway embankment between Oosterbeek and Wolfheze. Things were no better elsewhere. The Border Regiment and the remaining elements of the Airlanding Brigade had been under pressure on and off all day, and Divisional Headquarters received a report from 1st Airlanding Brigade Headquarters that the South Staffordshires in Arnhem had been reduced to 100 men and that in their area the rest of the force consisted of 150 men of 11th Battalion, forty from 3rd Battalion, 116 from 1st Battalion, thirty men of the Glider Pilot Regiment and a couple of Forward Observation Officers (FOOs) of the Royal Artillery. This force of 400-odd men was now extremely tired from continuous combat and perilously low on ammunition. It was certainly not an adequate force to carry out the sort of attack that might break through to the bridge. The final diary entry of the day was not encouraging either – Hackett's Brigade Headquarters and 156th Battalion had managed to reach their allotted rendezvous but lost contact with 10th Battalion.

6

D+3: WEDNESDAY 20 SEPTEMBER

The events of 19 September had not brought the main objective any closer. The Airborne Division was under intense pressure in Oosterbeek and could not possibly mount another offensive without immediate large-scale reinforcements. Also, the ammunition situation, although not yet critical, would inevitably become so before long.

It was painfully obvious that the Polish Brigade could not be dropped on the landing zones that had been decided in the planning stage of Market Garden. The area to the south of the Arnhem bridge had been rejected as a DZ for the first day's operations due to the expectation of high levels of anti-aircraft fire, but it had been assumed that the flak unit in the area would have been dealt with by 1st Parachute Brigade and that the Poles would have a safe place to drop. This had not happened and the area was firmly in German hands. Accordingly, Airborne Corps Headquarters in England had asked 1st Division to select an alternative site, and so the area to the east of the village of Driel had been agreed. The new DZ would have the advantage of a screen of woods along its eastern edge, which might provide some cover during the actual drop, and presumably 1st Division observers were confident that the proposed DZ was not occupied by German troops at the time the signal was sent to England. There was, however, always the possibility that, by the time the Poles landed, German troops would have taken over the strip of woodland, with a good field of fire and observation across the DZ. They would be difficult to remove. It is hard to see what, realistically, the Poles could be expected to achieve. If all went well they would have possession of a stretch of the south bank of the river and a perimeter around it, in which case the engineers of XXX Corps would be able to make a start on building a bridge across the Neder Rijn as soon as they and their equipment could be brought up. Additionally, the Polish arrival might draw some German attention away from the British, and it was certainly expected that Polish paratroops would cross the Neder Rijn into Oosterbeek. There were so many flaws in the proposal that it is hard to know where to start. Unless XXX Corps made a major breakthrough in overwhelming strength and at great speed – and there was little reason to believe that that was on the cards – the Poles were simply being put in harm's way to bring a rather modest level of relief to the hard-pressed 1st Airborne Division. Whether it would really make any noticeable difference to Urquhart's force is extremely questionable.

Quite how any significant numbers of Polish troops were to be carried over the Neder Rijn does not seem to have been given any serious thought at a senior level. Every Polish soldier crossing into the 1st Division area would mean one soldier fewer to protect the stretch of river bank that XXX Corps engineers would need for building a bridge. As if these problems were not enough, the Poles would be expected to form a perimeter on the south bank in an area with little cover and without the battalion and brigade assets that might give them a fighting chance against a strong German attack. It is difficult to avoid the conclusion that the British high command was prepared to risk a great many Polish lives to save a modest number of British ones.

Whatever conclusions were reached at senior levels, the state of affairs on the battlefield itself had continued to deteriorate. Captain

Faulkner-Brown and his fellow engineers were ordered to stand-to for 0430, but the early part of the day was thankfully quiet, until 0900 when a spate of heavy mortar fire opened up on and around the captain's positions, followed by infantry attacks to his left and right supported by two half-tracks. It is not clear whether these were troop-carrying Hanomags or vehicles mounting anti-aircraft guns, but clearly they were not just the heavy vehicles used for towing artillery. Reporting to Major Wilson's Independent Company Headquarters at Ommershof, Faulkner-Brown met a Dutch businessman, Mr Casterdijk, who had moved to his holiday home at Oosterbeek to avoid bombing at his usual residence in Rotterdam. It was Mr Casterdijk's son who would take the famous photo of a disabled Hanomag on Graaf von Rechterenweg.

Wilson brought Faulkner-Brown up to date with the situation. Colonel Frost's command was still holding out at the bridge, but the enemy was being reinforced steadily with infantry and armour and there was no prospect of relieving the colonel – in fact, the divisional perimeter around Oosterbeek was under pressure on all sides. Later in the day a self-propelled gun approached from the west along Graaf van Rechterenweg in support of an attack in company strength, and there was heavy firing on the King's Own Scottish Borderers at the 'White House' a few hundred metres away. The gun was driven away with PIATs and Gammon bombs but would undoubtedly return.

During another mortar attack, Captain Thomas was severely wounded and died shortly thereafter leaving Faulkner-Brown in charge of the party of Royal Engineers. Later in the day he was surprised to see General Urquhart being driven along Oranjeweg in a jeep – a dangerous undertaking since Oranjeweg was effectively the front line. Urquhart was en route to see Major Wilson at Ommershof. The jeep was being driven by Urquhart's aide-de-camp, Captain Graham Roberts, who found that he did not have quite enough room to turn the vehicle around, crashed into a boulder and was flung bodily out of the jeep. Urquhart's papers were in the jeep and could not be simply abandoned, so the senior NCO of the Independent Company, Company Sergeant Major Jimmy Stewart, ran out to recover them – an act of considerable heroism under the circumstances since the enemy was never far away and well supplied with snipers.

Overall, the situation on Wednesday morning looked rather bleak at Divisional Headquarters, and it did not look better anywhere else. Shortly after 0800, contact with 1st Parachute Brigade Headquarters at the bridge confirmed that the bridge itself was still intact and the defenders were still holding an area around the north end, but that they were in desperate need of reinforcements, ammunition and medical support, specifically a surgical team. Urquhart had become resigned to there being no prospect of making another attempt to relieve Frost's shrinking force and ordered his staff to inform 1st Parachute Brigade Headquarters that the only help they could anticipate was 'from the relieving force expected from the south'. This can hardly have been an inspiring signal, but equally it cannot have been a complete surprise. For more than two days, during lulls in their own battle, the bridge defenders had been able to hear the sounds of combat from the west. Those sounds, though, had not come any closer – evidently the Germans had the measure of the situation.

The news did not improve as the morning progressed. Brigadier Hackett's brigade – or rather what was left of it – had endured a bad night and shortly after 0800 reported that it was now held up in its attempt to break into the divisional area less than 1½km west of the Hartenstein Hotel. The Divisional Headquarters area came under attack from the east at 0930, and at the same time the Border Regiment were under attack from the west; the division was effectively surrounded and things were no better at the bridge.

By 0925, Divisional Headquarters had been informed that the bridge area was under heavy attack from enemy armour, and at about the same time a report came in to the effect that XXX Corps had been held up by a German strongpoint south of the Nijmegen bridge. The report stated that a new attack would be made at 1300, but that can have come as little consolation to Urquhart. Even if the attack was completely successful, and even if the Nijmegen bridge was captured immediately – and intact – the fact remained that XXX Corps would still be 15km away from the Arnhem bridge and there was no reason to think that the Germans would easily surrender that territory. It had already taken Horrocks' force nearly three days to cover less ground than had been planned for the first 24 hours of the operation.

Bombardment continued through the day. A report from 1st Brigade Headquarters in the early afternoon confirmed that the north end of the bridge was still under British control and that the defenders had inflicted considerable losses on the enemy. But the plight of the divisional area is exemplified by the fact that the divisional diarist was not aware that the Main Dressing Station in the houses around the Schoonoord Hotel had been in enemy hands for more than 2 hours, even though it was only a few hundred metres away. A signal received shortly after 1400, reporting that the Guards Armoured Division was trying to rush the Nijmegen bridge, was undoubtedly welcome news, but not, perhaps, particularly comforting or inspiring since it meant that XXX Corps was still some distance away.

At 1600, the Airlanding Brigade resumed command of the King's Own Scottish Borderers from 4th Brigade. They were now positioned south of the railway in and around the Ommershof woods at the northern edge of Oosterbeek, while the Border Regiment, Glider Pilots and elements of 9th Field Company RE retained their positions along the western aspect of the town. At the same time, there was, at last, some sign of an improvement in the situation. Part of an armoured reconnaissance unit from XXX Corps had reached the south bank of the Neder Rijn, and an hour later the second supply drop of the day took place. A first drop, shortly after 1400 that afternoon, had almost all fallen into German hands, but this time a greater proportion was gathered in, though nothing like the quantity required.

At 1745, Royal Artillery observers reported quantities of German tanks and transport on the eastern face of the perimeter. This was potentially a threat to the gun lines of 1st Airlanding Light Regiment around the Oosterbeek church, which would have a disastrous effect on the precarious situation of the division. The gunners had performed sterling service in breaking up enemy attacks. A successful thrust here might well capture or destroy the guns themselves, although, even if the guns were somehow extricated, there was really nowhere else for them to go.

This German mobilisation was, in any case, a serious threat to the whole southern aspect of the perimeter. A strong attack pressed home with vigour might cut the division off from the river. If so – and possibly with the loss of the artillery as well – Urquhart would have little option but to consider surrender or face the utter destruction of his command. The original target was still – just – in

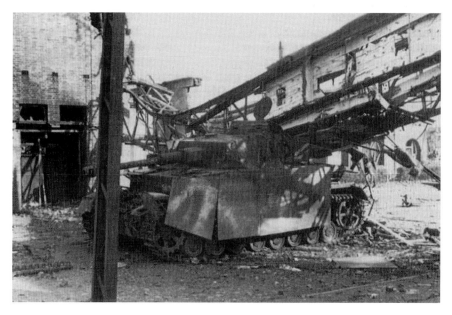

Destroyed Panzer IV tank.

German *Kübelwagen* and assault gun.

Oosterbeek church.

British hands, though the bridge defenders were already dependent on the arrival of XXX Corps for relief. There was nothing that the Airborne Division could do to help them. The battle was not yet lost, but continuing the fight once the river bank area was in enemy hands would achieve nothing other than an even greater loss of life.

Shortly before 1900, Brigadier Hackett arrived at Divisional Headquarters to report that what was left of his Brigade Headquarters and 156th Battalion were now within the divisional area. At 2400, the final divisional diary entry for the day confirmed that the Nijmegen bridge had been captured successfully, though by this time it must have been all too clear that there was little chance that the ground forces could arrive in time to prevent Frost's command being overrun. The Germans were perfectly aware that the Allied troops must capture the final crossing at Arnhem if they were to achieve the clear road that Montgomery needed for his plan to break through the Netherlands and into Germany. There can have been no doubt that the Germans would have thrown everything they could find into preventing XXX Corps' advance to Arnhem. The situation at the bridge was not promising. Frost himself was now out of action – he had been wounded in the legs at around 1330 and command had passed to Major Gough of the Reconnaissance Squadron. The ammunition supply was perilously low, with little or nothing left in the way of anti-tank capability. Indeed, four Tiger tanks and a reconnaissance vehicle had been able to cross the bridge and pass into Arnhem earlier in the day because Frost's men had nothing left to fire at them. The story of the determined resistance at the bridge was coming to an end – a force with no food, no water and, crucially, virtually no ammunition could not put up an effective fight. The situation was desperate for those still in combat and the plight of the wounded men in the basements and cellars was no better. During the afternoon, a local truce was arranged for the recovery of some men who were wounded but too isolated from an aid station and for the general transfer of casualties into

German hands. As they were marched or carried into captivity, they passed a long line of Mark IV tanks ready to finish the battle. One of the casualties – James Sim of 2nd Battalion's mortar platoon – was struck by the variable demeanour of the Germans. At one point he and his comrades were shocked to see a Dutch resistance man, who had been badly wounded in the hands, executed on the spot. Soon after that they witnessed a young paratrooper being shot for refusing to hand over his wallet. And yet, Sim was treated with compassion by two other German soldiers, one who gave him food from his own rations and another who gave him coffee – not a substitute, but the real thing, which was a rare and expensive luxury in wartime Germany. Sim was also struck by what he saw as an almost casual attitude to combat; as the prisoners were moved off, German soldiers called out 'good fight' and 'well fought'. Sim felt that they seemed to regard war in much the same way as the British saw football – as a sporting event – although it is probably more accurate to see the reactions of the Germans as statements of admiration for the tenacity and professionalism of their foes. Once the casualties had been evacuated, the fighting started up again. The British troops were not yet ready to give up their position, but it was increasingly obvious to both sides that the end was in sight.

7

D+4: THURSDAY 21 SEPTEMBER

The divisional diarist may have been left unimpressed by the first news he received on 21 September. At 0115, he recorded a message from the Phantom Unit informing the airborne force that the Guards Armoured Division was to go 'flat out at first light for the bridges at Arnhem' – an indication that XXX Corps was not yet aware that the railway bridge had been blown up on the Sunday afternoon and that the pontoon bridge had not been secured at any time (Pegasus Archive). The diarist would have been aware that there were good reasons for the Guards Armoured Division not to press on through the night – the tanks and other vehicles needed to be rearmed and refuelled, the men needed to be fed and the advancing troops would be vulnerable in the dark and might well become disorganised. Equally, it would have been obvious that failure to maintain any forward movement after dusk would give the Germans more time to reorganise their defences and bring up further troops, tanks and guns.

The diarist's next entry was even less promising. A patrol under Lieutenant Heaps had failed in an attempt to pass through the German lines and carry ammunition to the men at the bridge. Remarkably, although the division had informed the headquarters of

1st Airborne Corps that the supply drop had only produced enough food for one ration between every three men and that they were very short of ammunition for Sten guns, the ammunition supply generally was 'not unsatisfactory', but the division was now very short of water. The Germans had cut the water supply, but damage to mains pipes and to the buildings that housed the troops would have been a problem even if the supply had not been terminated at source.

At 0900, Urquhart held a conference of senior officers. He had decided to organise the perimeter into two commands. The eastern portion would be under the supervision of Brigadier Hackett and consist of the remnants of 10th and 156th Battalions, Thompson Force, which had been organised out of elements of the South Staffordshires, and various parachute units – men who had made their way back to the divisional area after the unsuccessful attempts to reinforce the bridge. On the northern and western aspects, Brigadier Hicks had what was left of his own brigade – the Brigade Headquarters, the King's Own Scottish Borderers (who had by this time been restored to Airlanding Brigade from Hackett's command), Border Regiment, the Reconnaissance Squadron and the Independent Company, as well as Royal Engineers and the balance of the Glider Pilot Regiment.

After several days of hard fighting and a great deal of bombardment none of these units was at anything like a reasonable combat strength. A great many men had been killed or lay wounded in the divisional area. A great many more had been captured or were in hiding in Arnhem having become detached from their units in the confusion of failed attacks or enemy action, or during the difficult processes of disengagement and night movements north of the railway line.

By 0915, two of Hicks' units – the Border Regiment and King's Own Scottish Borderers – were under attack. The Germans had briefly overrun one company of the Border Regiment at Heveadorp, but the situation had been restored by a counter-attack organised by

Wounded prisoners of war.

Major Breeze from men who had been driven from the position and a platoon of the South Staffordshires that had not been committed to the fighting in Arnhem. There was, at last, one piece of good news: the Airlanding Light Regiment had established contact with an artillery unit of XXX Corps – 64th Medium Artillery Regiment – and before long was calling in strikes around the perimeter with impressive effect.

The diary of 1st Airlanding Brigade (Pegasus Archive) records that the perimeter was contracted by moving the King's Own Scottish Borderers to the south and elements of the Border Regiment and other units under Major Breeze slightly to positions just a couple of hundred metres to the west of Oosterbeek church. The base of the

British medium artillery. Guns like these were instrumental in breaking up German attacks in the latter stages of the battle.

perimeter was now very narrow and therefore might at any time be compromised by a major attack.

The afternoon brought another supply drop, which, in the view of the divisional diarist, proved to be 'quite successful this time'. At 1715, Polish Brigade dropped to the east of Driel, and shortly afterwards the King's Own Scottish Borderers were subjected to another heavy attack and were reported to have been overrun. Half an hour later, a series of attacks with armour and self-propelled guns on the eastern aspect of the perimeter were broken up by impressively accurate fire from 64th Medium Regiment. Shortly after 1800, Divisional Headquarters received the reassuring news that the King's Own

Scottish Borderers had mounted a successful counter-attack to regain their positions lost an hour or so earlier, but were now down to just 150 officers and men – less than one-fifth the initial strength.

By 1840, news came that a German attack had recaptured the Main Dressing Station, followed by a report of an attack on the Border Regiment, which had been broken up with the aid of artillery action. The Commander Royal Engineers reported that he had dispatched a party to join Thompson Force and organised rafts to get Polish troops over the river, but also sent a signal to Airborne Corps Headquarters that there had been no contact with any elements of the division in Arnhem. The signal did not explicitly state that the bridge must now be considered lost, but the implication must have been clear. In fact, the heroic action had come to an end at around 0500. Instructions were passed for the men to try to slip or, if necessary, break through the German lines and rejoin the division, although even if the men had been fed, rested and properly equipped there would have been little chance of success. For exhausted, hungry soldiers with no ammunition there was no hope at all.

Faulkner-Brown's day had started with a mortar bombardment at dawn, but this had not been a precursor to an infantry attack. The combination of artillery or mortar followed by infantry – and armour when it was available – was standard practice as there was always a chance that the defenders would be shaken by the shelling or that some critical post had been destroyed. However, simply bombarding the perimeter units and then doing nothing at all was also common. As soon as the shelling ceased, the defenders would have to stand-to in the expectation that enemy infantry would appear at any moment. This meant that the men were continually under great stress, waiting for an attack that might come immediately, in a few minutes, an hour or not at all. In each case, the sudden silence and the atmosphere of apprehension took a toll on the physical and emotional stamina of men already severely tested.

Divisional transport after intense shelling.

At 0800, Major Perkins visited Faulkner-Brown, bringing him a small quantity of rations and news that the Germans had finally overrun Frost's command. Perkins toured the position, talking with the sappers in their trenches. While he was conversing with Lieutenant Evans, a mortar bomb exploded beside them, wounding Perkins in the throat and Evans in the elbow. By good fortune, Faulkner-Brown had some of the new miracle medication, sulphonamide powder, which had been given to his driver by a US airman. He applied it to the lieutenant's wound, an act that Evans would later credit with saving his badly damaged arm.

The rest of 4th Squadron were not really having an easier time in their position at the 'Sonnenberg' house. They had suffered a heavy mortar bombardment at 0915 and a strong attack by enemy infantry at 1100. The attack had been driven off, with casualties on both sides, but these incursions inflicted more wear and tear on the defenders than the attackers. The guns of the Airlanding Light Regiment and the mortar platoons of the battalions were in almost constant demand, and ammunition was not so plentiful that it could be used on speculative shots. It had to be reserved for breaking up attacks, so German troops could be reasonably sure that if they were not in contact with their adversaries they were unlikely to be subjected to bombardment. No doubt it was little consolation to men who were having to mount repeated attacks against determined defenders, but at least the Germans could hope to get a little rest from time to time, confident in the knowledge that the airborne troops were unlikely to mount any counter-attacks beyond those aimed at recovering a particular building or position that had been lost and now posed a local threat. Even if there had been Allied men available to mount an attack beyond the level of crossing a street or a narrow strip of ground, the troops were just too weary for offensive action.

Although the expenditure of ammunition had been heavy over the first few days of the operation, the supply had held up reasonably well. The troops at the bridge had run out of PIAT and Gammon bombs, and there had been local and temporary shortages, but by and large the troops had not been seriously hampered by a lack of bullets, grenades and bombs. The Airlanding Light Regiment had to be sparing with its shells, but this had not prevented the delivery of fire support. The situation started to become more problematic, though, on the Thursday. At 1005, an entry in the Divisional Headquarters diary shows that shelling and mortaring had set the main ammunition dump close to the Hartenstein Hotel on fire, so the general ammunition supply could no longer be considered 'not unsatisfactory' – as recorded in the Divisional diary the previous day – but would obviously become increasingly hazardous. A really successful supply drop would unquestionably help to ease the issue, but there was no reason to believe that future drops would necessarily be more profitable than those that had already delivered large quantities of materiel to the Germans. The perimeter was already very crowded – if a major supply of ammunition was procured, where was it to go? The dump that caught fire on the morning of 21 September had doubtless been selected as the optimum site, but until such time as it burnt itself out it would be a dangerous place to approach and clearly no use at all for the storage of flammable, incendiary and explosive material. The supply had reduced, but the demand had not. The fall in the number of men in action might, superficially, suggest that the consumption of small-arms ammunition would decrease, but in fact a greater proportion of the troops had equipped themselves with Sten guns so that they could deliver a more lethal response to German attacks. Ammunition for Sten guns, already at a premium, was now likely to become harder to find.

The troops could not possibly reduce the volume of fire. Appeals to 'make every round count' were a regular feature of 'O' groups but of limited value. Obviously, the enemy would make better progress if not subject to heavy fire and might deduce that the airborne troops were running low on ammunition. This may well have been in the minds of the German command anyway – airborne troops cannot

Drop in progress.

bring an unlimited supply of ammunition to the battlefield, and a large proportion of the supply canisters and panniers that had been delivered to the battle area had been collected by the Germans.

News of the fire at the main ammunition dump was probably not passed on to Harry Faulkner-Brown's Royal Engineers or to the other units around the perimeter. Any doubt about the security of the ammunition supply was hardly going to be a boost to morale and efficiency, and Faulkner-Brown's men – like their comrades – already had quite enough on their plate dealing with the enemy. At around 1530, yet another attack was successfully driven off, and there was little activity until 1800 when a German propaganda unit started playing the popular Glen Miller hit 'In the Mood' – a remarkable development given that this was exactly the sort of music that the Nazis strongly discouraged and saw as 'degenerate'.

War correspondent Alan Wood.

The music was followed by a call on the British to surrender, with blandishments about how well they had fought and how there was no dishonour in giving up the struggle now that the battle was lost. This did not cut any ice with the defenders, and after a short while the withdrawal of the propaganda unit was followed by an attack in strength, which was driven off, and another attack only an hour or so later that was similarly stopped.

It was during this period that the King's Own Scottish Borderers were driven out of their stronghold at the 'White House', as reported in the divisional diary. Faulkner-Brown saw one or two King's Own Scottish Borderers leaving the fight and was then confronted by 'a rather large' officer, who he told to return to his position. To Faulkner-Brown's surprise this worked perfectly well, but he thought the situation warranted reporting to Major Wilson and so made his way to Ommershof. There he found Wilson and the commander of the King's Own Scottish Borderers – Lieutenant Colonel Payton-Reid – sharing a restorative whisky. Payton-Reid immediately set off to the 'White House' to restore the situation, which he did by directing a 'spirited' attack to reclaim the building. However, the King's Own Scottish Borderers had now been reduced to a shadow of their former strength and may have had as few as 100 men still able to fight. As the day came to an end, Faulkner-Brown was surprised by how confident he felt – an indication that his men were still in good heart.

As night fell, Faulkner-Brown was called to a meeting with Wilson, who told him that there were concerns about how fragile the perimeter was, that Germans were able to slip thorough at various locations and that General Urquhart intended to reduce the size of the perimeter and thereby shorten the line that needed to be held. The King's Own Scottish Borderers, the Independent Company, the party from the Glider Pilot Regiment and Faulkner-Brown's sappers were in real danger of becoming isolated. He was ordered to stand by to pull his men back to the Hartenstein Hotel, where they would come under the command of Brigadier Hackett. Tired beyond measure, Faulkner-Brown made his way down the Oranjeweg to the centre of the divisional area and met up with his new superior, who told him 4th Brigade had only 100 men fit for action.

Faulkner-Brown was shown the position he was to hold and told that he was to mount a counter-attack if the Germans penetrated the perimeter through the group of small hotels and large suburban houses that were now the Main Dressing Station a couple of hundred metres from Divisional Headquarters. At around midnight, his men – two officers and fifty-five other ranks – joined him. He took them to their new post but told them not to dig in until morning, when they would have a clearer picture of fields of fire and the optimum locations for their trenches and foxholes. Around the battlefield the struggle continued in fits and starts, but with odd interludes that must have seemed slightly surreal. Sergeant Ronald Gibson of the Glider Pilot Regiment relates that the unit chaplain managed to organise a local truce for an hour on the north-west shoulder of the perimeter. There had been a good deal of activity through the day, including a lengthy action while the Border Regiment cleared a stretch of woodland and wounded men from both sides lay scattered among the trees. A medical officer in SS uniform came to the unit command post to finalise arrangements and was outraged when a British officer there pointed out the security risk of allowing an enemy soldier to come into their lines and that the enemy might break the truce at any moment. The officer declared that the Germans did not go in for breaking their word. Gibson's comment on this reflects what seems to have been the general view of such situations throughout the battle – 'So far as our experience taught us, this was perfectly true. They were very particular in such matters of etiquette and were chivalrous to our wounded' (Ronald Gibson, 1956).

8

D+5: FRIDAY 22 SEPTEMBER

As Captain Faulkner-Brown's engineers settled down – so far as that
was possible – for what remained of Thursday night; their neighbours
on the northern aspect of the perimeter were also leaving Ommershof.
At 0100, the Independent Company formed up to start the move
southwards to a new position under Brigadier Hackett. Ron Kent
became aware that one man was not at all enthusiastic about exchanging
his foxhole for unknown territory and had to be 'encouraged out of it
with his section sergeant's Colt automatic in his ear' (Ron Kent, 1979).
The move was completed without any interference from the enemy,
though one soldier was lost. The company rested for about 2 hours
at or near 4th Brigade Headquarters and took up its new positions.
Number 1 Platoon took over the house across the road from the
Schoonoord Hotel, where the company memorial stands today, and
the other two platoons and the Company Headquarters established
themselves in houses on the south side of the road at 0500. Not long
after this. Lieutenant Colonel Stevens, the senior staff officer with
the Independent Polish Parachute Brigade, arrived at Divisional
Headquarters to inform Urquhart that two battalions and the Brigade
Headquarters had landed on the south side of the river, but had not
been able to make a crossing.

This can hardly have been news to Urquhart; the arrival of the aircraft and the spectacle of the jump, not to mention the sound of German activity around the DZ, would not have passed unnoticed. Urquhart must also have been all too aware that the Poles would have little, if anything, in the way of boats, and that even if boats could be found or rafts constructed the Poles would only be able to cross in small numbers and only under cover of darkness. A short while before dawn, Divisional Headquarters was informed that the Guards Armoured Division would not be advancing from its present position between Nijmegen and Arnhem, but that 43rd Division would attack 'at first light'. This was followed by another signal from Airborne Corps Headquarters, declaring that 43rd would 'take all risks' to relieve the Airborne Division that day and that its efforts would be directed on the ferry that normally ran between Driel and Heveadorp.

Yet again this showed a lack of understanding of the situation. The ferry had not been taken into consideration at any stage in the planning process and had in fact been lost – or released from – its moorings. Even though the ferry itself was not available, the ferry landings on the north and south banks would have been useful for getting amphibious vehicles and boats into action, and they had been recognised as valuable assets for the delivery of the Polish Brigade once the decision had been taken for it to be landed at Driel. This might have been the case, but the company of the Border Regiment that had been posted on the Westerbouwing hill, overlooking the ferry, had been driven off their position on the morning of Thursday 21 September.

The day had been busy throughout the divisional area. At 0900, a force of infantry, supported by flamethrower tanks, had attacked the Royal Engineers at 'Sonnenberg'. The engineers beat off the threat and disabled one of the tanks, only to have to face another attack at 1600, which was also thwarted.

Yet more bad news had reached Airborne Division Headquarters at 1335. Airborne Corps Headquarters informed them that less than half the aircraft carrying the Polish Brigade had actually reached the DZ, and therefore the brigade was seriously under-strength, though it is hard to imagine that Urquhart had not already learned this from Lieutenant Colonel Stevens.

By late afternoon, Urquhart was in contact with Polish Brigade Headquarters and arrangements were made for some of Sosabowski's men to cross the river that night. The crossing was to be attempted a little way upstream from the ferry route, which was dangerously close to German positions to both the east and west of the perimeter. Sosabowski, however, was willing to take the risk, even though it was thought that no more than 150 men might be carried across the Neder Rijn before daybreak. The operation went ahead, and shortly before midnight 1st Airlanding Light Regiment (which the divisional diary describes as 'Thompson Force') was able to report that some Poles had been brought into its position, though clearly this minor accretion in strength was not going to make any real impact on the course of the battle.

The continual noise of shelling and small arms wore men down; they could not sleep and it became increasingly dangerous to leave their positions to answer calls of nature or to find food, water and ammunition. Even so, there could be quiet periods. Sergeant Gibson and his comrades stood-to before dawn and waited for shelling or an attack, but there was no noise or movement in their corner on the north-west aspect of the perimeter until mortar bombs started to fall at 1000. Later in the day Gibson would find himself reading – of all things – a copy of the *Daily Express*, which had arrived in the previous day's supply drop. A banner headline, 'Dempsey Does It Again', and a map showing the progress of XXX Corps to Nijmegen suggested that the relief of the Airborne Division was imminent, perhaps only a matter of hours. The thought was dispelled very shortly afterwards when Gibson overheard an officer telling a senior NCO that he had just attended a brigade commanders' conference where he had been told that the division was now reduced to less than half of its strength, that there was a serious ammunition shortage and that General Urquhart had warned XXX Corps that they might well be overrun completely if they were not relieved within 48 hours.

The conference had taken place at Divisional Headquarters. Adjacent to this, in the middle of the morning, Captain Faulkner-Brown and his men had a curious experience. A press photographer arrived at the captain's position with some airborne troops and staged pictures of these men moving through a series of ruined buildings adjacent to the Hartenstein Hotel. The event provoked an understandable display of annoyance from the sappers but amused the captain.

Shortly before noon, Faulkner-Brown was called to the Hartenstein Hotel to meet the Commander Royal Engineers. This was something of a risky undertaking since German snipers had infiltrated the divisional area and he had to make a dash across open ground, but did so without incident. Lieutenant Colonel Myers told him of the previous attempt to ferry Poles across the river in rafts made from jeep trailers, which had not been a success, and that XXX Corps was now at Nijmegen. Myers also told him that he had been selected to organise another attempt that night. Faulkner-Brown was ordered to take some of his men to the rectory beside Oosterbeek Old Church (the house of Kate Ter Horst) and do whatever he could to get more Poles across the river that night. Accordingly, that afternoon he took one of the few remaining operational jeeps to collect two inflatable boats from a house just south of the Hartenstein Hotel. The captain found that the house was now an overflow area for the less seriously wounded, and he also found a 'bright and cheerful' chaplain, who was able to tell him that there were in fact six boats and an RAF dinghy that had, presumably, been salvaged from one of the many aircraft shot down. While they spoke, a mortar bomb exploded nearby wounding the chaplain in the throat. Faulkner-Brown thought the chaplain had been killed outright, but he was later found a few hundred metres away from where he had been hit. It seems most likely that this helpful officer was Captain H.G. Irwin of 11th Parachute Battalion. Faulkner-Brown chose a dozen men and loaded them into two jeeps along with the boats and dinghy and another officer with a radio to provide a link to Divisional Headquarters. The party made their way down to the river where he dismissed the jeeps and told the drivers to return before dawn.

After dark Faulkner-Brown crossed the river and made contact with some Poles, informing them that he intended to string the boats across the river, attached to a signal cable at six locations, and draw them back and forth across the water, carrying small parties of Polish soldiers. Unfortunately, the signal cable proved to be too fragile for the task and the boats had to be paddled against the strong current.

British Army radio set.

Jeep-mounted radio set. (Courtesy of Philip Reinders)

Officer's compass found in Kate
Ter Horst's garden. (Courtesy of
Philip Reinders)

Radio operator.

It was a long night at the end of a long day – in fact several long days.
Faulkner-Brown had put several men on sentry duty, but lying still in
the dark they naturally kept falling asleep and he had to periodically
kick their boots to wake them up. He also had serious difficulties
with a Polish officer who – perhaps understandably – was unhappy
at the slow progress, but whose interruptions were not making
things any easier. Eventually, in sheer exasperation, Faulkner-Brown
had to take out his pistol and tell him that if he did not '…f★★★
off, I'll have to shoot you' (Harold Faulkner-Brown, 2006). This did
the trick, and the officer disappeared. The number of men being
carried into the perimeter was almost inconsequential, and the night
was coming to an end, so sometime after 0400 Faulkner-Brown was
forced to bring the operation to a halt as daylight approached.

9

D+6: SATURDAY 23 SEPTEMBER

At 0355, the first entry of the day in the divisional diary declared that fifty Poles had been brought over the river and put under the command of 1st Airlanding Brigade. Brigadier Hicks was doubtless very happy to have them, but it was a meagre addition to his depleted and exhausted force. Nobody was any more tired than Captain Faulkner-Brown after his night on the river. In the early morning, he reported back to Brigadier Hackett and, for the first time since he had gone to bed on the previous Sunday night, took his boots off. He also had the good fortune to find a sofa and got his head down, only to be woken shortly afterwards to find that the house was under artillery fire. Brigadier Hackett wanted the captain to go immediately to Divisional Headquarters and tell them that 4th Parachute Brigade Headquarters was being shelled. On his return, he reported back to the brigadier, and in the course of their conversation Hackett told him, 'Houses are a snare unless we can keep the self-propelled guns around the corner' (Harold Faulkner-Brown, 2006). This might appear curious since buildings should provide cover, but they also constituted more easily identifiable targets for artillery pieces than trenches and foxholes in gardens. A house was likely to attract men anxious to get into cover, but it might easily be set on fire with shelling. Furthermore, there was a limit to how far the barrel of a self-propelled gun or tank could be depressed, making it very difficult to fire directly at a ground-level trench.

Hackett was now very short of troops and he ordered Faulkner-Brown to a new location to reinforce Major Powell, who was now in charge of what remained of 156th Battalion. Faulkner-Brown dutifully led his men to the position, where he found that Powell's force – two officers and about thirty other ranks – was fighting across a narrow patch of back gardens filled with sheds and hen houses. The position was very confined, and Powell simply had no space in which he could deploy the sappers. He told Faulkner-Brown that he would have to find his own place in the battle. Powell may have been the only officer on the battlefield who had – however briefly – more men that he could effectively use. Throughout the night, the effort to get Polish soldiers across the river continued, but it was a difficult business and only about 200 men had joined the perimeter when dawn put an end to movement.

Divisional diary entries through the rest of the morning tell of steady shelling and mortaring, a series of attacks around the perimeter and that the majority of men had had no rations for 24 hours. An entry at 0945 states that the ammunition supply was now dangerously low but that a cache might be delivered from leading elements of 43rd Division, which had arrived on the south bank of the river. Another entry at 1105, however, indicated that no supplies had been received. Half an hour later, the diary recorded that an attack on a company of 1st Border Regiment had been repulsed, but that the Poles serving beside it had incurred heavy casualties – some 50 per cent of their number.

As the British – and now Polish – troops became increasingly tired, the Germans became increasingly frustrated. It was obvious the battle was lost and that the spirited resistance of the airborne troops was going to achieve nothing more than a higher toll of

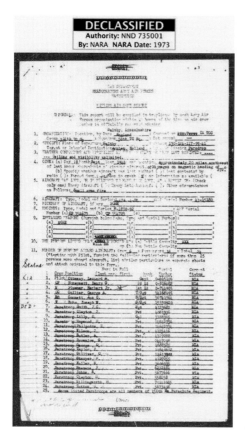

Flight record of personnel of 156th Battalion. (Courtesy of Philip Reinders)

casualties on both sides. At 1300, 4th Brigade Headquarters reported that a German officer had approached under a Red Cross flag and demanded the withdrawal of the troops in houses around the Main Dressing Station area and that if this were not carried out he would shell the hospital. He seems to have been dissuaded and accepted a compromise, whereby he would not fire on the hospital if the British agreed not to fire from houses in its immediate vicinity.

The report casts the German officer in a poor light, but he could hardly be expected to demand anything else. If his men were under fire from buildings adjacent to the hospital, they would inevitably fire back. Furthermore, it might well be effectively impossible for the Germans to identify precisely which buildings held active, if exhausted, airborne soldiers and which held wounded men – at least thirty of whom were in fact Germans who had been taken prisoner over the preceding days.

Another attack on the Border Regiment was made shortly after 1330 – in battalion strength apparently, though it must have been exceptionally difficult to make such an assessment under the circumstances. The attack was repulsed with the loss of a German tank.

Another supply drop was made at 1605, but very little materiel was collected. A considerable proportion fell directly into German hands, but collection was now a problem in itself. The divisional area was vulnerable to sniper fire from outside the perimeter in a number of places and several snipers had managed to slip inside the perimeter as well. Additionally, collapsed buildings or fallen trees now blocked many of the roads, so the few jeeps that were still operational could not move around the perimeter to collect the canisters and panniers.

German prisoners of war.

Throughout the day there had been some modest encouragement for the men on the ground. An improvement in the weather had allowed the RAF to mount a number of strikes against enemy concentrations and – perhaps more significantly – engage German aircraft and prevent them from making attacks on the beleaguered airborne troops. There was, though, a limit to what the pilots could do – the opposing forces were very close together and the risk of friendly fire incidents was high.

Late that night – at 2345 – Lieutenant Colonel Mackenzie returned to Divisional Headquarters from a trip across the river. He had been to the headquarters of both the Polish Brigade and 43rd Division. He had given details of the current situation of the Airborne Division to both Horrocks and Browning and also attended the 'O' group of 130 Brigade of 43rd Division and been told that the Poles would start to make their way across the river that night and were to be followed by 130 Brigade either later that night or the following night.

10

D+7: SUNDAY 24 SEPTEMBER

The divisional area was repeatedly shelled and mortared through the night in what was becoming a distressingly familiar pattern. The perimeter was large enough to present a target that could be shelled safely as far as the surrounding German troops were concerned, though no doubt the odd round fell short or overshot the target. Equally, the perimeter was now so small that every shell that did fall inside it might well find a target, and even those that did not would be damaging to the morale of the Airborne Division. Apart from preventing sleep, the shelling was discouraging men from relocating or improving their trenches and foxholes, or from going in search of supplies.

The shelling also made it increasingly difficult to recover casualties and get them to dressing stations, and the plight of those casualties was made worse by the sheer proximity of the makeshift hospitals to the fighting. Understandably, there were problems with interpretation of what was, or was not, a legitimate target. At one point, the chaplain of 1st Airlanding Light Regiment – Captain Thorne – and Bombardier Stan Boldon had to run out from the Ter Horst family residence waving a Red Cross flag at a Tiger tank, which was just about to fire on the house, and tell the tank commander that the house was being used as a dressing station. The tank commander called for a superior, and shortly thereafter a German officer arrived to hear what the chaplain had to say. Once the situation had been explained, the officer agreed that the house would not be fired on but – not unreasonably – demanded that the chaplain should make arrangements to remove a machine gun team from the building. After the battle, Mrs Ter Horst was adamant that no machine gun had been fired from her home, but Thorne was equally sure that the gun had been there, as he had issued a direct order – apparently for the one and only time in his career – for it to be removed.

The Ter Horst house, Oosterbeek.

At 0535 that morning a piece of news was relayed from outside
the perimeter by the Phantom reconnaissance unit, which had
its own wireless connection to the War Office in London. Thirty
kilometres to the west, a formation of Major General Thomas' 43rd
Division – 214 Brigade – had attacked to clear the town of Elst
during the previous evening, but enemy action had prevented the
progress of 129 Brigade. Current thinking was that 130 Brigade
would make an assault river crossing with two battalions during the
night, slightly to the west of the Heveadorp ferry points, followed by
Royal Engineers who would construct a class 40 bridge to enable
the tanks of XXX Corps to come into the battle. At the same time,
214 Brigade would advance roughly along the line of the railway on
the south side of the river and thereby secure the flank of the Polish
Parachute Brigade's drop zone to the east of Driel.

By 0620, a Polish liaison officer had reported to Divisional
Headquarters at the Hartenstein Hotel with the news that there was
now one battalion of Poles (less its headquarters company) on the
north side of the river. This was hardly the sort of major addition to
the divisional strength that was required if the perimeter was to be
maintained in the face of German activity. A battalion might sound
like a useful force, but the term is somewhat misleading in this
context since a parachute battalion had only three rifle companies
and was really not much more than 300 men. Also, dozens – perhaps
scores – of the Polish troops who had crossed the previous night
had already been killed or wounded. All the same, it had been quite
an achievement to get men across the river at all. The mere fact
that it was even attempted speaks volumes for the determination of
Major General Sosabowski and his colleagues. Two hundred of these
newcomers were assigned to the north-east aspect of the perimeter
under Brigadier Hackett, while the remainder were sent to join
Brigadier Hick's command and reinforce the perimeter's western
face. Less than an hour later Hackett was wounded and replaced
by the commander of No. 1 Wing of the Glider Pilot Regiment,

Lieutenant Colonel Murray, who had flown Urquhart's glider to the battlefield a week earlier.

A report sometime after 1500 informed Divisional Headquarters that Germans were demanding that British troops should move away from the Main Dressing Station area at the crossroads to the west of the Hartenstein Hotel or else they would shell the buildings. Although this could easily be construed as callous blackmail, it is important to remember that the Germans were fighting a battle. An enemy with a less well-developed set of military ethics would have simply carried out the shelling without warning. Given the proximity of the hospital buildings to the fighting generally, and to the route that a German attack must take if it were to penetrate to the centre of the divisional area, it was inevitable that at some point the Main Dressing Station crossroads would become a combat zone – in fact it did so more than once.

Equally, it is important to understand that however much he would have liked to protect the wounded from further suffering, Urquhart really had no choice but to order the medical staff to stay where they were. The perimeter was so narrow that there was no place to which the wounded could have been evacuated that would have been any safer, and the loss of the buildings would create a greater weakness in the string of trenches and houses that comprised the north-east shoulder of the divisional area. Little more than an hour later the matter had been partially resolved: the Germans had captured the central part of the Main Dressing Station, and the Assistant Director Medical Services (ADMS) – the senior doctor had reported to Urquhart that the Germans were now evacuating some of the British casualties who could be safely moved out of the buildings and taking them to Arnhem as prisoners of war.

The fighting at the Main Dressing Station still continued, though. At 1900, the Independent Company reported that it had reached an agreement with the Germans – it would evacuate a key building next door to the Main Dressing Station and, in return, the Germans

250 Coy RASC (Airborne Light)
APO ENGLAND.

Dec 30th 1944

Dear Mrs Jones.

Thank you for your letter in reply to mine of Dec 18th. The enclosed sum of money is sent on behalf of all members of the Company as a contribution towards the cost of Prisoner of War Parcels. We hope to send a further donation when funds permit.

The address you sent has been passed on to his friends, who will no doubt be writing to him soon. I hope that you continue to receive good news.

Yours sincerely,

(J.H. Gifford) Major RASC.

250 Company Royal Army Service Corps made a collection for their comrades taken prisoner at Arnhem. (Courtesy of Philip Reinders)

British medical staff after being taken prisoner.

would remove a self-propelled gun from the crossroads so that it would not attract fire that might hit the dressing station. This agreement, however, also removed the vehicle from what was a very useful firing position.

British medical staff.

Other than the action at the Main Dressing Station, a day of severe fighting had made little impression on the perimeter. A number of local attacks had driven the defenders from one position or another, but most of these had been recovered in counter-attacks. However, the situation was becoming more and more difficult by the hour. Although the casualty rate was not too steep, it was still far more than Urquhart could afford, and those men who had not been wounded were exhausted and hungry. Small-arms ammunition was getting scarce, and the shortage of bombs for the PIATs was 'becoming a serious handicap' (Robert Urquhart, 1958). Most of the anti-tank guns were out of action, either through battle damage or the lack of ammunition and crew. Once the PIAT ammunition ran dry, German armour could prowl the streets with virtual impunity, putting shells into every strongpoint until the whole of Oosterbeek was either flattened or ablaze.

The last divisional diary entry for the day was a bleak one. Airborne Corps Headquarters in England informed Urquhart that there could be no supply drop the next day due to bad weather over the Channel. This must have been a bitter blow to the general. His men had been fighting for a week to retain objectives that they should have been able to turn over to the ground forces in a day – or two at the most. They had made a stalwart defence against a powerful and determined enemy. It was a hard enough task in itself; but to continue to do so without adequate food, water, medical supplies and ammunition, and for the rather questionable purpose of keeping a toehold on the banks of the Neder Rijn, was beginning to smack of sheer cruelty.

11

D+8: MONDAY 25 SEPTEMBER

Yet again there was nothing positive for the divisional diarist to record in his first entry of the day. At 0605, the Commander Royal Engineers returned from a hazardous trip to the south bank of the river with a letter from the commander of 43rd Division, Major General Thomas, which informed Urquhart that the previous day's plan to attack across the river and make a crossing to the west of Arnhem had now been abandoned. It also said that the Airborne Division would now withdraw across the river by arrangement with 43rd Division, at Urquhart's discretion – the point at which he felt the division could not 'hang on' any longer (Robert Urquhart, 1958). It should have been absolutely clear that the point had already arrived. If XXX Corps were not going to make a crossing into the Oosterbeek perimeter, there was absolutely no point at all in keeping the airborne troops in action for a moment longer than was necessary. Any evacuation programme would have to wait for nightfall, but there should not have been any question about the importance of it proceeding at the earliest opportunity. There is a genuine question as to where General Browning was in all this. He should certainly have given the instructions to Urquhart himself, simply as a matter of common professional courtesy, quite apart from operating within the proper chain of command. Leaving it to Thomas was not so much a delegation of authority as an abdication of responsibility.

The Commander Royal Engineers was also able to tell Urquhart that an infantry battalion – 4th Dorsets – had crossed the river about 1km beyond the western face of the perimeter, but had not made contact with the division. The Dorsets had been accompanied by three DUKWs – amphibious trucks carrying ammunition and other stores for the division – but there had been no sign of their arrival in the divisional area. It is hard to see what Urquhart was supposed to make of all this. His division had not been relieved when it should have been. The possibility of such a failure in war is a fact of life, and Urquhart was a realistic man, but now his division had apparently been discarded by the corps commander. Browning had not given Urquhart any sort of explanation of the situation or of his own analysis and conclusions, which is all the more puzzling given that he really did not have anything else to do. Most corps commanders are busy fighting a wider battle, but Browning had been no more than a privileged spectator since the moment he boarded a glider back in England on 17 September. He had reduced the airlift capacity of 1st Airborne Division by exactly the amount of gliders and aircraft that were required to take him and his headquarters to a battle in the Netherlands. He had attended a number of high-level briefings and 'O' groups to which he could make no useful contribution, and now that the fight was over he went out of his way to avoid contact with the man whose division had suffered dreadfully in pursuit of an operation of which the practicalities had always been highly questionable at best. It was simply insulting to Urquhart, both professionally and personally. If he was not furious beyond measure, it is hard to see why.

To make matters even worse, another battalion of infantry had been thrown into a fight with no real plan or purpose. Whatever it did and however hard the men fought, they could have no meaningful impact on the precarious situation of 1st Airborne Division. The Dorsets had suffered heavy losses to no useful purpose and were now on the wrong side of the river, surrounded by the enemy. Even if they were able to fight their way through to join the Airborne Division, a few hundred more infantrymen were not going to tip the balance of the battle, and the three DUKWs – even loaded to the maximum capacity with medical stores, food and ammunition – would scarcely replenish the airborne troops, most of whom by this time were probably even more severely affected by the lack of sleep than by hunger.

Urquhart had been given discretion over the timing of his withdrawal, but in practice he had no choice in the matter. His men could not possibly cross the river in daylight and he could not fight on for another day without risking the total destruction of his command, with terrible loss of life. Browning had not so much given Urquhart discretion, as avoided taking the personal responsibility of actually issuing an order to withdraw.

Clearly the division had to be evacuated, and equally clearly it had to be evacuated as soon as possible. Shortly after 0800, Urquhart passed word to General Thomas that the withdrawal – to be known as Operation Berlin – had to go ahead that night. A short while thereafter, the liaison officer for the Dorsets arrived at Divisional Headquarters. He was able to inform Urquhart that two companies of his battalion were now near to the position of the 1st Airlanding Light Regiment around the Oosterbeek church and that the other two were close to the ferry landing on the north bank of the river and therefore still some distance from the west face of the divisional area. The officer also told Urquhart that these two groups of men were not in contact with one another, that he himself was not in contact with his battalion headquarters – nor presumably the support elements of the battalion such as the mortar platoon – and that he did not know the whereabouts of his battalion commander. All in all, it was not proving to be a good day – and that day had only just begun.

At 0940, a further signal was sent to Airborne Corps Headquarters back in Britain. The signal reported Urquhart's understanding that some stores – medical supplies, rations and a quantity of ammunition – had been sent across the river, but that enemy action had prevented them from reaching the perimeter. The signal also reported the division's effective strength as being down to 2,500, plus the men of the Polish contingent, and drew attention to the continuing shortage of supplies of all kinds, but most particularly the critical shortage of ammunition for the guns of 1st Airlanding Light Regiment. At 1040, Urquhart held a divisional conference and issued orders for Operation Berlin to be put into action that night.

As the day progressed, there was, it would seem, little for the divisional diarist to add. The shelling and mortaring went on as they had done for some days, and there was continual, sporadic action all around the perimeter and, increasingly, within the perimeter, as the loss of positions to enemy action and bombardment made it easier for small parties to slip between the houses. At 1800, the diarist made his first entry since 1030, referring to an attack that had dislodged the handful of men from 156th Battalion who were still in action and recording the presence of the enemy at several locations, which meant that most of the units in the division were now cut off from those to their flanks or rear.

During the afternoon, Captain Faulkner-Brown was called to Divisional Headquarters. He and about half a dozen other officers were met by Lieutenant Colonel Murray of the Glider Pilot Regiment who had taken over command of the eastern aspect of the perimeter. Murray explained the basic plan for Operation Berlin. The route was to be marked by two-inch tracing tapes – an item of standard Royal Engineers equipment used for marking paths through minefields or marshes. Withdrawals from the north of the perimeter were to start at 2100 hours, 4th Brigade troops were to be ready to move off at 2145 and crossing was to begin at 2200. The officers were ordered not to tell the men until 1600 at the earliest.

Any instruction for a withdrawal tends to make soldiers more concerned to keep their heads down for fear of becoming a casualty in the very last hours of a battle, and there might be a diminution of effort and a loss of concentration if it were known that everyone would be abandoning their positions before long. What was much more of an issue was the possibility that an attack or an enemy patrol might result in a man being captured and interrogated and then revealing the plan.

A number of students of the battle have suggested that Operation Berlin was premature; that it would still have been possible to force a crossing and gain a bridgehead over the Neder Rijn and press on with Market Garden. But in fact all the senior officers who were in a position to make a judgement accepted that the operation had run its course. The only thing to do was to extract as much of 1st Airborne Division as possible. Clearly there was no way of evacuating the wounded, many of whom were unfit to travel under any circumstances – and certainly not on foot to the river

A German patrol.

and then in a difficult crossing by small boats. Arrangements were made for coloured tracer rounds to be fired to the east and west of the perimeter to indicate the area from which men would be collected by the boats of the Canadian and British engineers, and for the airborne soldiers to withdraw by stages to the river bank. Urquhart's plan was inspired by his knowledge of the withdrawal of British and Australian troops from Gallipoli during the First World War, an operation that he had studied in some detail for an examination early in his career. The men on the northern face of the perimeter had the furthest to travel to make their way toward the river, they would be followed by the men on either flank so that the east and west faces of the perimeter would be steadily rolled down to the Neder Rijn.

The individual German soldier may not have cared too much whether the defenders managed to escape destruction – and all the more so if it meant that he personally would not have to take part in a string of actions to winkle the British out of every house and foxhole in Oosterbeek. This, however, was certainly not a view that would have been acceptable at more senior levels. The battle of Arnhem/Oosterbeek had certainly been won, and it was the first German victory against the British for some time, but the victory would be that much more impressive if the 1st Airborne Division was utterly and completely destroyed.

As things stood, that destruction might well still be achieved. At much the same time that Faulkner-Brown was attending the meeting at Divisional Headquarters, a determined German attack with armour and artillery support came close to cutting off the base of the perimeter at the river; another such attack might well succeed. Faulkner-Brown briefed his NCOs at around 1600. He ordered that the remaining water should be shared out: half for a brew of tea – or just for drinking – and half for shaving. Presumably, he wanted his men to look as presentable as possible when they got to the south bank of the Neder Rijn.

Battle damage to the Old Church in Oosterbeek.

Postcard showing the aftermath of the Battle of Arnhem, September 1944.

The order to withdraw affected the men in different ways. Most who were still able to do so boarded boats or attempted to swim across the river. Captain Thorne, chaplain to the Glider Pilot Regiment, was briefed by Major Gex, who had taken over command of the artillery regiment in place of the wounded Lieutenant Colonel Thompson. He told Thorne that an evacuation would take place during the night of 25–26 September, but – like the medical staff and the other chaplains – he decided to stay with the wounded men.

Battle damage in Arnhem, possibly in the vicinity of the St Elisabeth Hospital.

Throughout the day, a considerable force of artillery had been assembled to the south of the river, and a heavy barrage was opened up on German positions around the perimeter at 2100, with the twin objectives of dissuading the Germans from investigating the situation too closely and disguising the noise of the withdrawal. The rain that had fallen intermittently throughout the afternoon became heavier, which was a further advantage in achieving both objectives. Faulkner-Brown led his men down to the river bank past the Ter Horst house and a great many bodies – the Ter Horsts would return several months later to find fifty-seven men buried in their garden. He found an orderly but long queue of men waiting to be picked up and decided to find a shorter one, so he led his men along the bank and had the good fortune to find an abandoned assault boat complete with paddles. Considering it his duty as an engineer to do what he could to hasten the evacuation, Faulkner-Brown decided to start a 'ferry service'. He made one trip across the river and was just about to set out again when a Canadian engineer officer insisted that his men would take over the task and that the captain should make his way to the concentration area.

12

D+9: TUESDAY 26 SEPTEMBER

The divisional diary records that Operation Berlin was discontinued at 0530, as the dawn would render the process unfeasible – the Germans would have excellent fields of fire across the river and the risks were just too great. Despite the sterling efforts of the engineers, there was still a queue of about 300 men on the north bank. Arrangements were made for boats to be sent over to collect them when night fell, but as the Germans were already starting to move into the perimeter it became all too clear that many – in fact most – of these men would become prisoners during the course of the day. There was certainly no possibility that they could have formed any kind of defensive position that would have protected them for the daylight hours and allowed them to be picked up when darkness fell.

By 1200 Divisional Headquarters had moved from the rendezvous at Driel to Nijmegen, where the men of the division were given tea, rum, food and a blanket from the stores of 130 Brigade. The men were undoubtedly glad to get the hot stew, but some were probably surprised at the small portions on offer. This was a matter of policy. The overwhelming majority of the troops had had little or nothing to eat for some days and could have made themselves ill by overburdening their shrunken stomachs.

British prisoners of war marching off to captivity.

British prisoners of war.

That afternoon, Urquhart held a conference with his staff to make arrangements for billeting and the issue of clothing, and also for establishing contact with the division's seaborne 'tail', which was now at Nijmegen. The original plan had called for the Airborne Division to continue to fight on as conventional infantry once the Arnhem objective had been secured, and the 'tail' had brought the hundreds of vehicles and tons of equipment that the division would need for that role. Now the only thing missing was the manpower. Approximately a quarter of the division had been pulled out across the Neder Rijn and nearly a fifth were dead on the battlefield. The remainder – more than half – were now prisoners of war.

The following day Urquhart held another conference of his senior officers so that they could report on the progress of the reorganisation of their units. It must have been a rather hollow meeting, as virtually every part of the division had lost so many men that any kind or reorganisation would be meaningless. The same conference addressed the possibility that the remnants of the division might be evacuated to Britain by air from Grave. By doing so, they might escape the forthcoming visit by General Browning, who was to address the troops at 1700. In the final entry for the day, the diarist recorded that Lieutenant Colonel Mackenzie had issued orders for the divisional motor transport to move to Diest in Belgium, a plan that only extended to the vehicles of the 'tail' since the rest of the division's vehicles had been destroyed or captured in Arnhem and Oosterbeek.

13

WHEN THE SHOOTING WAS OVER

The fighting around Arnhem and Oosterbeek had inflicted a heavy cost in men killed and wounded. Nearly one in five of the men of 1st Airborne Division had been killed – an enormous loss by the standards of modern combat. More than 6,000 men had been taken prisoner, many of whom were wounded, with a substantial number wounded for a second or even third time as they lay in the makeshift casualty centres in Oosterbeek or at the bridge. It would be easy for this to be seen as evidence of wilful cruelty, or even just negligence, on the part of the German Army, but that would be far from fair. The constricted nature of the Oosterbeek pocket and the perimeter at the north end of the Arnhem bridge meant that it was inevitable that shells, bombs and bullets would find their way into the hospitals; there was no means of preventing it. One German officer did approach under a flag of truce to announce his intention to attack and enquire whether the British hospital facility, which he knew lay in the path of his advance, might be removed to the rear to avoid further injury. His sentiment was honourable, but there was nowhere for the wounded to be evacuated to – apart from outside the other edge of the perimeter and thus behind German lines. On more than one occasion truces were arranged so that wounded men

Temporary graves before the final development of the Arnhem cemetery. (Courtesy of Philip Reinders)

could be taken into German captivity rather than have to endure further shelling; there was really no more that the Germans could have done to alleviate unnecessary suffering. In a more conventional combat situation the majority of these men would have been evacuated to dressing stations and then to hospitals behind the lines, so avoiding the eight months of captivity they had to endure.

Operation Berlin had been quite successful in the sense that most of the men fit to move were extracted successfully. By sheer good fortune, the weather had taken a turn for the worse and Operation Berlin was carried out in the pouring rain, which made it difficult for the Germans to identify what was happening. If the night had been clear, the German observation posts and patrols would have realised that the British were making a withdrawal and so mounted attacks to cut off their escape route. This would have surely caused more casualties among the exhausted airborne troops and more men to be taken prisoner.

Some thought had been given to the possibility of building a bridge into the Oosterbeek perimeter, and General Sosabowski, among others, had raised the possibility of XXX Corps forcing a crossing of the Neder Rijn downstream to form a new bridgehead and to relieve the Airborne Division. In all probability, neither of these were genuinely practical propositions. The business of constructing a bridge was not beyond the capacity of the engineers – Commonwealth troops, for instance, had built a bridge of similar length in Burma – but to do so under constant fire was a different matter. There would probably have been heavy losses, with no guarantee of success. Even if such a bridge could have been built in time to help the men in Oosterbeek, the troops of XXX Corps were almost as tired as the airborne soldiers. They might have been able to get across the river, but whether they could have forced their way through what was, by this time, a considerable German force, was by no means certain.

As ever when an operation goes badly wrong, there was a raft of safeguards put in place to protect the reputations of the men who had made the crucial decisions and, in the tradition of armies everywhere, to find a scapegoat. The enormous gamble had come to nothing and nobody would want to take responsibility for the first real Allied defeat in the campaign.

It would have been difficult – and grossly unfair – to blame Urquhart. No commander is perfect, and there were various shortcomings within the division that may not have originated with him, but for which he had responsibility as the General Officer Commanding. Urquhart had put himself out of contact with his headquarters for a lengthy period at a crucial juncture in the battle, but the same misfortune could have struck any commander who wanted to get out and about to see what was happening. Given the extensive failure of the signals equipment, it is hardly surprising that he should have gone off in search of the units that were marching on the primary objective. His absence caused various problems and he was not on site to deal with others as they arose, but it is hard to see what he could have done to have a material effect on the progress of the operation. While Urquhart was stuck in Arnhem, Hicks made the only decision he could – to send the South Staffordshires into Arnhem to bolster 1st Parachute Brigade. With the benefit of hindsight, there was one possible option that Urquhart could have chosen, but it would have been a risky one. Hackett's brigade was scheduled to land even further from the target than the initial drop zones, and Urquhart could have taken the daring course of diverting the King's Own Scottish Borderers from the task of protecting 4th Parachute Brigade's drop and committing them to the fighting in the town. This would have caused all sorts of difficulties in relation to the duties of 21st Independent Company, who would have been unable to set out the recognition signals, though it is reasonable to assume – since the aircraft had no difficulty in identifying the zones – that the drop would have gone ahead. Hackett's brigade might have had to face an opposed landing, but this is not at all certain. Certainly, the Germans had captured maps showing the proposed drop zones, but they could not be sure that the maps were actually entirely reliable and not a partial ruse, or that the drop zones could not be changed – they, after all, had no means of knowing that the Airborne Division had failed to establish communication with its higher command. In that light, it is quite credible that the Germans would have committed all the men they could to dealing with the enemy that had already arrived and preventing them from achieving their objective, and that therefore the opposition on the landing zones would not have been particularly significant. Hackett would have been left out on a limb and, since he had no better luck with signals than Urquhart, would have faced a choice between setting up his own perimeter and awaiting developments or trying to make his way to join the rest of the division. It is hard to imagine how he might have done anything other than the latter, so the German troops to the north and west of Oosterbeek could see that they had an aggressive enemy force to their rear. Since many of these troops were not of the highest quality, it is unlikely that they would have found that a comfortable situation. Sending units of the Airlanding Brigade into the town would have put Hackett's force at risk, but that might have been justified if it had brought about a large and secure perimeter, including the road bridge. However, there was no certainty that it would. Street fighting tends to swallow up troops at a phenomenal rate, and the strength of the airlanding units could easily have been dissipated to no good purpose. Even if Urquhart had been at his headquarters during the crucial period, he would have had no grounds for making such a radical change to the divisional plan. It would not have been clear to him – in the same way that it was not clear to Hicks that the advance had stalled so very badly until, at best, well into the evening of 17 September, nor that the renewal of the advance in the early dawn of 18 September would fail to have the desired effect. This being the case, and even if minded to do so, Urquhart would not have been justified in diverting any more of the available troops to the advance into Arnhem until – at the earliest – the late morning of 18 September, by which time the King's Own Scottish Borderers and the Border Regiment were at least half a day's march from the objective, even if they encountered no opposition at all. There is no guarantee that reinforcements from those two regiments would have had the impact necessary to change the course of the battle.

Even on the most optimistic basis, there was no real possibility of getting reinforcements into the fight until late on 18 September, and by that time the German defence was well established and in good heart. The Germans had already prevented any reinforcements from reaching Frost's 2nd Battalion at the bridge, where both the 1st and 3rd Battalions and the South Staffordshires – already diverted from the defence of the landing zones – had been thoroughly mauled in exactly the kind of battle of attrition for which airborne forces are specifically not designed.

Signals operators.

Whatever decisions Urquhart made on the ground, there is a strong argument that success was all but impossible from the moment the drop zones had been chosen. Urquhart cannot be held responsible for that. He had tried but was unable to persuade the 'air' side of the undertaking to deliver his division to more appropriate sites. That was really not his decision to make, thanks to the structuring of responsibility. It had long been general policy for the air planners to have both the first and final say on the subject.

The argument that 4th Brigade, and the other units and elements to be landed on 18 September, would have faced little or no opposition is, at best, questionable. If the Allied planners had identified the open terrain around Wolfheze as a potential landing zone, there is no reason to assume that the German planners could not have done the same. In any case, regardless of where exactly the second lift elements were to land, the Germans had ample warning of their impending arrival. The convoys of thousands of aircraft could hardly be disguised as they flew over territory that was still under German occupation. Curiously, the German garrisons that still held ports on the coast saw the airlifts but seemingly did not pass the information up the chain of command. Abandoning the landing zones and ordering every unit to move on Arnhem would have been beyond Hick's authority and a tremendous risk for the second and third lifts. Even if – a very big 'if' – the landing had gone ahead without serious damage to the second lift, it is not clear that the general situation would have improved. Furthermore, the units of the second lift might well have been stopped in their tracks and prevented from joining the rest of the division, in which case Urquhart, when he rejoined his headquarters, would have been faced with the prospect of commanding a division in three locations – the landing zones, the bridge and Oosterbeek – separated by enemy forces and with precious little communication between them.

The argument that the delay of the second lift due to weather conditions in England had a critical effect on the progress of the overall battle is better founded, but by no means secure. It is true that 4th Brigade and the rest of the lift would have been in action rather more quickly, and that the Germans would have had fewer assets on hand to confront them, but the general tenor of the fighting was already established. Even if the 1st Brigade and the South Staffordshires had arrived as scheduled, when they hit the ground – several miles from the objective – they had already fought to a standstill, not once, but twice. Their casualties had been heavy and the men were already exhausted. Even if 4th Brigade had made the best possible speed towards the target area, the Germans would have had plenty of time to reinforce their line. Also, even before Hackett's men were due to arrive, the Germans had already defeated attempts by 1st and 3rd Battalions and the South Staffordshires to clear a path to the objective. It is true that the landing zone would have been abandoned once 4th Brigade was on the ground and that the King's Own Scottish Borderers and Border Regiment battalions would have been able to retire towards Oosterbeek, but they could hardly be withdrawn from the battle and thrown at Arnhem without exposing the balance of the division to German attacks from the west, and running the risk of losing the proposed resupply drop zone into the bargain. The fact that the supply zone was never actually secured is neither here nor there. If all of the division's infantry assets had been applied to the advance into Arnhem there would not have been much of a force left over to seize it, or if it had actually been secured, there would not have been enough men to prevent it being overrun by a German counter-attack.

To all practical intents and purposes, once the decisions had been made to land the division to the west and north of Oosterbeek, and to spread its delivery over three days, Urquhart's hands were tied, and, in his absence, Hicks did all he could under the circumstances. There was no real divisional reserve as such and the best Hicks could do was to assign the South Staffordshires to support what was already a failed attack, and then, when 4th Brigade arrived, dispatch one of Hackett's battalions in the general direction of the bridge in the hope that it would turn the tide of the battle.

Hicks' decision has been dismissed, by a variety of commentators, as wishful thinking and unwise given the general situation, but that is a very unfair assessment. For one thing, Hicks had little intelligence material on which to base his decisions. For all he knew, the German forces that had put a halt to the advance of 1st and 3rd Battalions might have done so by a very narrow margin, and potentially the enemy might be extremely vulnerable to a renewed attack. Indeed, in those areas where the airborne troops were no longer in contact with the enemy, there might be few – if any – German troops at all. It would not have been a great surprise if they had been withdrawn to mount an attack against Frost's battalion in the hope of recovering possession of the bridge, in which case the battalion detached from Hackett's command might fall on their rear, achieve a linkage with

Frost and form a corridor that would enable more troops to reach the objective. Equally, Hicks could certainly not afford to simply accept the situation as it stood, and had he done so he would certainly have been the target of a great deal of criticism after the battle was over.

There would undoubtedly have been a body of opinion claiming that 'just one more push' against the German defenders would have made all the difference to the outcome. Hicks did all that he reasonably could to make the operation a success, but he really did not have the resources to snatch a victory. His decisions did not go down particularly well with the commander of 4th Brigade for obvious reasons, and Hackett's famous phrase to the effect that he had arrived to find a 'grossly untidy' situation was not unjustified. This was, though, hardly Hicks' fault, and Hackett did, in fact, support Hicks' decisions. In practice, nothing Hicks did had any real effect on the course of the fighting, but there was little else he could have done – had there been some other course of action it would doubtless be well known to students of the battle and would have been discussed and dissected endlessly over the last seventy years.

If there was little Hicks could do in the absence of his superior, there was really nothing Urquhart could have done either. He – or Hicks for that matter – could, perhaps, have ensured that 11th Battalion was committed to the battle rather earlier in the day. In Hackett's opinion the unit was 'cruelly misused' since it had to wait around for some hours at a critical juncture of the battle before being ordered to move on Arnhem. That period of enforced idleness certainly did nothing to help the situation, but it is not really obvious that an earlier advance would have had a major effect on the progress made towards the objective. Equally, it is not altogether clear what reasons there might have been for delaying the unit's advance at all, since the 11th Battalion was the only unit that could be diverted from its own objectives to support the attempts of Brigadier Lathbury's brigade in Arnhem itself. As it was, the battalion moved only after dark and towards a battle for which there was very little worthwhile intelligence. It was sent – with elements of several other units – to do whatever it could to move matters along, but there was no definitive plan, and the battalion could count on nothing in the way of artillery support before dawn at the earliest, even assuming that such support would be available after daybreak and that reliable communications could be established with the gunners of the Airlanding Light Regiment. Even if those assumptions were proved to be true, there was no guarantee that the gunners would not be engaged on other tasks at a particular point. Securing the bridge was, of course, the primary objective and – in an ideal world – all other operations might have been overridden to provide artillery support for 11th Battalion as and when it encountered a viable target. If the battalion were making good progress it might reasonably have priority over the demands of some other unit en route to the bridge, but who was to say whether the 11th Battalion attack was the most viable at any given moment? On top of that, the needs of 2nd Battalion – who were at the objective itself – would have to take priority to avoid the prospect of 11th Battalion or the remnants of 1st or 3rd Battalion or the South Staffordshires arriving at the objective only to discover that the Germans had already overrun it.

Hicks might simply – and understandably – have been hesitant to commit the only available asset without the sanction of the divisional commander. Had Urquhart sanctioned it, he would have had no freedom of action to influence the battle on his return to his headquarters. It may have seemed at the time that there was a good case for waiting for more intelligence from the battlefield. If one or other of the units in Arnhem made a decisive breach in the German lines and established contact with Frost's battalion at the bridge it would be vital to have a fresh unit that could be committed to reinforce the men at the objective. It was perfectly possible that an attack by 11th Battalion could become mired in street fighting and be brought to a halt, while a clear passage had been achieved just a few hundred metres away. Had that been the case and the operation had failed, there would have been seventy years of criticism for committing the nearest thing to a true divisional reserve prematurely and in the wrong part of the battlefield.

When Urquhart returned to his headquarters, the battle was far from over, but the general framework was already well established. Hicks has been criticised for making decisions which, ostensibly, restricted Urquhart's choices, but Hicks really had no means of knowing when Urquhart might make his appearance, or even that he would return at all. For all Hicks knew, Urquhart might well have been killed in action and be lying in a bombed-out building, at a roadside or in the woods, with nobody any the wiser.

As far as can be ascertained, Urquhart would not have made radically different commitments. He does not appear to have been critical of Hicks' actions and it seems reasonable to conclude that he would have pursued a very similar agenda. There does not seem to be any reason to assume that Urquhart would, therefore, have had any appreciable impact on the proceedings.

There is a perfectly good case to be made that Urquhart had not acted wisely in leaving his headquarters in the first place. Although his frustration at the failures in communication and his concern that the leading elements of the attack were not making rapid enough progress is perfectly understandable, it is not clear that he could realistically hope to exert much influence on the course of the action. Indeed, at one point both he and Lathbury were doing nothing more than casting a shadow over the leading company and platoon commanders. Those officers had enough to do in fighting the battle without senior officers breathing down their necks. Urquhart should, of course, have been at his headquarters in case he failed to receive whatever information became available. As it happens, the poor performance of signals equipment – largely a matter of soil conditions – would not have provided him with much material through the evening of 17 September and the following night. He would, of course, have been more aware of the delay to the second lift, and better informed about the extent and nature of the German forces in front of him, if not hiding in an Arnhem attic, but it is hard to see what use Urquhart could have made of the information. The first that anyone on the ground knew about the delay of the second lift was when it did not arrive, and there was absolutely nothing that Urquhart or anyone else could do about it. In Urquhart's absence, Hicks and Hackett had 'an almighty row', but it is hard to see any practical, viable alternative to the course of action that they took. The presence or otherwise of Urquhart would have made no difference to the communications situation, to the scale of force available or – most importantly – to the reactions of the Germans.

Perhaps because almost all of the troops of 1st Airborne Division were British, and because almost all of the literature on the battle has been produced by British writers, there has been a strong tendency to focus on 'where the British got it wrong' rather than 'how the Germans got it right', and this has, in a sense, led to an unbalanced

Montgomery, Hackett and Urquhart.

popular perception of the battle. This is not uncommon in battle studies of any period. Much more attention has been given to General Lee's defeat at Gettysburg or Edward II's defeat at Bannockburn than to the victories of General Meade or Robert I of Scotland at the same battles. This may be natural or even inevitable, but it does obscure a large part of the story. Whatever the shortcomings of the Arnhem plan — and they were many and at all levels — the operation might still have been a success if it had not been for the swift and effective reactions of the Germans.

It is all too easy to follow the actions of the first day on a map and see a picture of battalion engagements, but in fact progress in even a very large battle in such close country really depends on success in a great number of small actions. When we look at the experience of this or that battalion on the march to its objective, we should constantly bear in mind that in reality, at any one moment, the vast majority of the battalion would have been strung out in a column along the road over several hundred metres — perhaps as much as a kilometre or so. Even a modest level of resistance encountered by the leading section or platoon could bring the whole unit to a halt, while other elements — rifle platoons, the machine gun or mortar platoon, perhaps anti-tank guns — were being deployed to overcome the obstacle.

If this had not been uppermost in the minds of the planners before the operation, it was certainly obvious to the Germans, or at least to SS Sturmbannführer Krafft. After the battle he wrote a very detailed — though somewhat exaggerated — report that sheds a good deal of light on the course of the battle throughout the afternoon and evening of 17 September. He evidently had no fear of blowing his own trumpet, but the essential tenor of the report was perfectly true. Although his command was a reserve depot and training establishment, and though it included a number of experienced officers and NCOs who had been selected specifically to impart their skills to the recruits, some of the men were not fully trained soldiers. Krafft had disposed his modest force with considerable skill and was

Mortar team in action.

able to communicate the situation to his men with good effect. They were not to fight to the last man and the last bullet, but to cause as much delay as possible at every opportunity. The force at his disposal was not large, but he used it with remarkable efficiency. Few officers at his level – in any army – would have had the confidence, insight and determination to make the decisions that he did on 17 September. In very short order he identified the objectives of the enemy, analysed the strengths and weaknesses of his dispositions and the general situation of the German forces in the area, and put the correct solution in place.

Krafft did more than simply establish a defensive line to try to impede the progress of the enemy. He instituted several attacks in line with the perceived wisdom that the best way to disrupt and frustrate an airborne attack was to 'drive right into it'. Krafft's attacks – and his defensive measures, for that matter – did not, in fact, inflict all that much damage in terms of casualties, but they did cause a great deal of delay and confusion, and his men were able to disengage on the evening of 17 September knowing that they had done a good job. Urquhart's observation that airborne troops cannot be acclimatised to the battle in any meaningful way since they are, more often than not, plunged straight into it has a very real relevance here, as does his comment that in the initial phases of a battle soldiers can tend to be – in his words – 'bullet-shy'. Given the nature of bullets, it is hardly surprising that anyone would be shy of them, but Urquhart's meaning was that in the first contacts with the enemy, a unit can often be held up for a lengthy period out of all proportion to the scale of the opposition. In part this is was due to inevitable weaknesses in training. Battle drills are practices honed to perfection in the classroom and on exercises, and – as a rule – will be of great value. Men know what they are to do and when and how to do it, but conditions in the field may require a more proactive and less formalised approach. This is particularly true for airborne forces in a hurry to reach an objective. It might be standard practice in this or that situation to deploy the mortar platoon or call for artillery support, but in a time-critical scenario there may be no opportunity to do so.

It is important to remember that although many of the men of 1st Airborne Division had been in combat in North Africa and Italy, a large proportion of the individuals who took part in Market Garden had never been in battle, and many of those who had seen action had not spent much time fighting. A proportion had seen action in the past – particularly in North Africa and in the early stages of the Italian campaign – but they were far from being a majority of the members of the division. Also, the environment in which they had fought had been very different; the close terrain of the Arnhem–Oosterbeek–Wolfheze area was a world away from the battlefields of Tunisia or Sicily. The division contained many veterans, but it was not really a veteran division.

The Airborne Division was also hampered by sheer bad luck. There was certainly evidence before the operation started that there were stronger German forces in the Arnhem area than had originally been anticipated, but not enough to indicate the presence of an armoured corps. The 9th and 10th SS Panzer Divisions had been seriously depleted over the preceding weeks, but they remained formidable formations. Weakened as they were, they still constituted a major concentration of enemy forces, although they would have been that much weaker if action had not been taken to retain armoured vehicles that should have been on their way back to Germany. There were also the matter of SS Sturmbannführer Krafft's reaction in the first few hours of the operation and the failure of resupply and reinforcement drops due to bad weather. The latter should have been considered as a possibility, though, as it turned out, it probably would have made no significant difference to the outcome of the battle. The same cannot be said about Krafft. The misfortune for the Allies of having an exceptionally active enemy commander – albeit at a relatively low level in the command chain – quite so close to the drop and landing zones, and quite so well positioned to offer effective resistance to the first wave of movement toward the principal objective, had an enormous impact.

By chance, Krafft's troops had been training in the Wolfheze woods on the morning of 17 September and were not, therefore, scattered throughout the vicinity enjoying a little time off – although many of the German troops in the Arnhem area were doing just that. Equally, since they were a training unit, they had a wide variety of equipment, including mortars and machine guns. There was not an unlimited amount of ammunition, and although this does not seem to have been a critical issue through the afternoon of the first day of the battle, Krafft must have been aware of the limitations of his command.

Krafft resisted the temptation to try to take on too much and decided that he did not have a sufficient force under his command to form a defensive line from the railway and road to the north-east of Wolfheze all the way to the banks of the Neder Rijn. He deployed troops from just north of the road to a point almost as far as the road junction where Major General Kussin was killed, and thus there was little to prevent Frost's battalion from reaching the bridge at dusk. However, if Krafft had spread his troops more thinly they might well have been unable to prevent the advance of the 1st and 3rd Battalions from passing through the town to the bridge, and so Lathbury's original brigade plan could, therefore, have been completed. As it turned out, the single battalion at the bridge was a hard nut for the Germans to crack, though it would have been very much harder had the entire brigade – or at least the bulk of it – been able to form a perimeter around the objective. That does not necessarily imply that 1st Brigade would have been able to carry the south end of the bridge during the night of 17 September. Crossing a bridge under fire is extremely hazardous, and Frost's attempts to force a passage that night were not successful. However, it is worth bearing in mind that Frost's resources were scant and he could not afford to lose any more men in mounting a succession of attacks; potential losses, though, would have been somewhat less of an issue if the whole brigade had been present.

Krafft may have gilded his account of his activities on the first day of Market Garden, but his actions were instrumental in unhinging what should have been – and was expected to be – a rapid advance by all three battalions of 1st Brigade to capture the Arnhem road and rail bridges and a variety of other objectives, all of which were really quite peripheral to the purpose of the operation. This was, of itself, a major weakness in the overall plan and a major benefit to Krafft and his men. At every juncture where the advancing paratroop units met the enemy, there was no means of committing an overwhelming force that could brush aside the level of resistance that Krafft's small force could offer. His unit has often been described as an NCO school and consisted, therefore, of men of proven commitment and ability. This was not the case; it was a reserve and replacement centre.

They were not organised or equipped as a combat unit, and despite the fact that Krafft undoubtedly put the best gloss he could on his own performance and that of his men, his decisions and actions on 17 September constitute an exemplary piece of soldiering by anyone's standards.

As we have seen, the attempts to push more men through Arnhem to join Frost's command on 18 September came to nothing and exacted a heavy price, though it is hard to see what else Urquhart could have done. His mission was, after all, to take the objective, not to fight a defensive battle in and around an obscure little town. That, however, is the position he found himself in by the end of that day. The partial success of Frost's force was offset by the fact that the 1st, 3rd and 11th Battalions and the South Staffordshires had been very roughly dealt with, many of them making their way back to the division along the bank of the Neder Rijn in some disorder, where they were gathered together by Lieutenant Colonel Sheriff Thompson and eventually reorganised into Lonsdale Force. By the morning of 19 September it should have been clear that there was little prospect of renewing the march into Arnhem and that the division was now engaged in a fight for its survival, some miles from the objective.

Whether this was fully understood at the headquarters of 1st Airborne Corps, XXX Corps, 2nd Army or 21st Army Group is irrelevant. The ground troops were still far enough away for there to be nothing that they could do to intervene. Urquhart's division was already in an extremely dangerous situation. Unable to communicate with the outside world, he had no means of arranging for the supply drop location to be changed, and although the stock of ammunition was not yet an issue, it would soon become so.

With no other choice, Urquhart was now reduced to conducting a defence of Oosterbeek with a badly depleted force and no clear idea of when he might expect to be relieved, resupplied or reinforced. The latter was not really considered an option by either Airborne Corps or 21st Army Group. The commander of 52nd (Lowland) Division,

South Staffordshire Regiment, survivors of the battle. (Courtesy of Tim Poole)

Brigadier Edmund Hakewill-Smith, made it clear to Browning that he was prepared to take his men into the battle by glider even though they had no suitable training, only to be told – by Browning – that the situation at Arnhem was not so serious as all that and that 52nd Division would not be required. Gallant as the proposition was, it was not really a viable option. There was little space in the perimeter and nowhere that could be used as a major landing zone for a glider force. The only realistic means of reinforcing the perimeter was to get men across the Neder Rijn once XXX Corps reached the river.

That would be a major challenge in itself. Without a bridge, fresh troops could only be added in penny packets, and with little if any armour. By the time XXX Corps did get to the Neder Rijn that challenge was already an extremely questionable proposition. The troops in the perimeter were exhausted to the point of collapse and could hardly be expected to continue the fight for another two, three or more days while reinforcements were ferried in. Any additional troops – at least to begin with – would have to be transported across the river at night or face inordinately high casualties from artillery and small-arms fire from either side of the crossing. Even if such an operation were successful, in the sense of delivering enough men to secure the Oosterbeek perimeter, it is hard to see what real benefit would have been gained. The ground forces would have had to put several thousand men across the river to relieve the airborne troops at a time when XXX Corps was already short of infantry, and in the face of increasing German strength. Horrocks might commit a large force and still be driven out of an area that could only become a useful bridgehead if his engineers got an opportunity to build a bridge.

Once it became clear that the fight at the bridge had come to an end, and that XXX Corps would not be able to force a crossing into the perimeter, the best that Urquhart could hope for was that the thousands of wounded might be evacuated and therefore not become prisoners of war. If this had been achieved, a great deal of suffering would have been avoided, but only at a heavy cost to the men of XXX Corps. Horrocks might have been able to secure the potential bridgehead, but the Germans were now firmly embedded around the perimeter, and breaking out from that encirclement would almost certainly have proved costly. He would have needed to commit more forces than he could afford to put at risk, and it was possible that even if he crossed the Neder Rijn and broke through the surrounding German forces, his position might not be materially better. The purpose of Market Garden had been all too clear from the first day of the operation, and the Germans enjoyed the luxury of more than a week to take measures to prevent the rapid Allied advance into Germany that might have been achieved had Market Garden gone to plan.

From a German perspective, the prospect of XXX Corps relieving the Airborne Division continued to be a possibility right up to the point of evacuation. The British and Canadians were known to have effective engineering departments – Commonwealth engineers had built at least one bridge of a similar scale in Burma under severe conditions. In terms of achieving the original goals of the operation, building a bridge was not really a viable proposition other than as a temporary measure until such time as the Arnhem bridge could be secured. From the Allied perspective, it was not at all clear that that bridge could be captured in the sort of timescale required to press ahead with the original goals, although that was not necessarily obvious to the German high command. Even if they had been utterly confident about continuing to contain a heavily reinforced perimeter, the Germans could hardly be sure that the Allies would not pursue the operation.

The Allied command was well aware that German efforts to provide troops, armour and artillery for the defence of Arnhem had proved effective, and there was no way of telling how many more could be committed to the battle. It is perfectly possible that even if the Arnhem bridge had been secured by the advance of XXX Corps, Horrocks might have ended up with nothing more to show for the operation than a pocket bridgehead on the far side of the Rhine in Arnhem and possibly a second one at Oosterbeek.

There was also the chance that the Germans might decide to demolish the Arnhem bridge. Field Marshal Model had expressly forbidden that option in the early stages of the battle, but it should have been apparent to him that there was no realistic prospect of staging the level of counter-offensive that he wanted. Even if enough troops and materiel were found, there was a more pressing need for them on the Eastern Front to slow the advance of the Russians and in the west to tackle the US armies.

It is too simple to discard Market Garden as an outright failure, in the sense that there were really two operations in concert – one airborne and one land based. General Lewis Brereton's claim that 'Market' had been a 'brilliant success' (Lewis H. Brereton, 1946) was something of an exaggeration, but almost all the objectives had been secured. The bridge over the Son river and the Arnhem railway bridge had both been demolished, though this had only been achieved by the narrowest of margins. The Arnhem road bridge may not have been captured, but the airborne forces had, broadly speaking, fulfilled their part. There was nothing that Urquhart, Gavin, Taylor or Browning could have done to accelerate the advance of XXX Corps. Montgomery's aim of having XXX Corps relieve the Airborne Division in the space of 24 hours was extremely optimistic, but if this had been accomplished within 48 hours – the time that the Airborne Division would be capable of holding the objective as Browning claimed to have told Montgomery – then XXX Corps would have found the north end of the bridge securely held by Frost's command. In those circumstances, it is hard to see how the Germans could have prevented the link-up on which the plan depended.

Whether 2nd Army – and XXX Corps in particular – would have been able to continue its advance thereafter is open to question. Supplies and manpower issues were a major challenge, and the troops were extremely tired. That said, a breakthrough 60 miles deep would undoubtedly have made some impression on the morale of the German Army. It would be simplistic, though not unthinkable,

Rebuilding the railway bridge. (Courtesy of Hugh Muir)

to assume that even such a dramatic incursion would have provoked another outbreak of panicked retreat among the German troops, but it would surely have had a disruptive effect on the physical structure of the army and on the provision of supplies as well as undermining confidence – not to mention the likely boost to the general morale of the Allied forces.

There can be no question that if the operation as a whole had been a success, Montgomery, Horrocks and Browning would have been more than happy to accept the plaudits for a daring mission executed with skill and determination. Since it was a massive strategic failure, they all had little to say about it afterwards – indeed, the whole operation gets rather superficial treatment in Montgomery's memoirs, which are fairly extensive on the other great operations of his career. This is not particularly surprising; in a sense there was not much for any of them to recount – an operation was staged and it failed. That is part of the reality of command in wartime. Operations must be planned and carried out with limited knowledge of the enemy's resources, situation and intentions. Only a fool would expect that every operation is likely to bring the advantages that the commanders hope to gain. Nor is it unreasonable for commanders to focus on their successes and great challenges. They are not 'on oath' when writing their memoirs or, by and large, constructing detailed historiographical analyses of their active careers. They are not historians, just men recounting specific aspects of their past.

What is less acceptable is a campaign to pass the blame for failure on to others, and there was certainly some shifting of the blame in the aftermath of Market Garden. Various officers – with or without the co-operation or assent of their colleagues and superiors – made consistent and largely successful attempts to tarnish the reputation of General Sosabowski. The most blatant example is Browning's report to the Imperial General Staff (the most senior body of the British Army) on Sosabowski's attitude and performance before and during the battle. It consisted of little more than character assassination, and Browning's assertion that his opinions and observations would be backed up by Major General Thomas and Lieutenant General Horrocks smacks of collusion.

Given that Sosabowski was one of the few officers – and the only senior officer – to consistently express doubts about the wisdom of the operation, criticism of his conduct on the battlefield was unfair as well as dishonest. A man of exceptional professional abilities, he did his level best to draw attention to the many weaknesses of the overall plan – not least by pointing out that the Germans could hardly be expected to just sit around and watch the operation unfold. When the orders were issued and his men committed to the battle, Sosabowski did everything that he possibly could to make it a success. The attacks on his personal competence, and therefore on his brigade, were a demonstration of the mentality of the British Army at its very worst.

It is open to question whether Urquhart was really the optimum candidate for the post of divisional commander, and several writers have explored this in the past. However, it is difficult to see what any other officer could have done that was radically different or likely to produce a successful outcome. In the unlikely event that it had proved possible to concentrate 1st Airborne Division and the Polish Brigade in the manner that the plan envisaged, the Germans would not have had to divide their resources between the action at the bridge and the fighting around Oosterbeek. To keep the proposed supply drop area secure, the division would have faced an increasing amount of armoured attacks and artillery concentrations, and they might well have failed. The fortitude of the airborne troops enabled them to retain one end of the bridge beyond the 48 hours Browning had stipulated as the maximum period that the division could hold it, despite the failure of most of the formation to get to the objective at all. It is far from clear, however, that even the whole division could have secured both ends of the bridge, and even less so that it could have held its position until XXX Corps arrived. Once the battle settled into a defensive pattern at Oosterbeek, Urquhart conducted himself in an exemplary fashion. It is hard to see how he could have done any better in the face of such strong opposition had he been ensconced in Arnhem rather than in a small town a few miles away.

The defeat of 1st Airborne Division – which the German news and propaganda operation naturally described as an elite force and the cream of the British Army – was certainly a coup and a boost to the morale of the German Army. But victory at Arnhem did not really profit the Germans. Defeat did prevent the Allies from making a fast advance across the Netherlands, and thereby possibly from breaking into Germany, but it is not impossible that XXX Corps could have been stopped before it travelled far from the Neder Rijn. The German victory made no real difference to the outcome of the war in the sense of provoking an opportunity to achieve an armistice and a negotiated peace settlement. The Allies had suffered a setback, but they had not really been repulsed. They ended up with a salient 60 miles long and going nowhere in particular, but they had only really been beaten in a divisional action, and their armies had not been crippled. In any case, the Allies were certainly not prepared to entertain any notion of a political conclusion to the campaign if it meant leaving any of the German ruling caste in place. Roosevelt, Churchill and Stalin had agreed on the need for a total and unconditional surrender. At least one German commander saw the victory as a strategic disaster. Failure to race across Germany and bring the war to an end in the autumn of 1944 brought about the Soviet occupation of Berlin and eastern Germany. That proved to be a heavy price to pay for what was – in terms of the European campaign as a whole – a relatively minor battlefield victory. A strategic failure for the Allies did not really constitute a strategic success for the Germans, and although a tactical victory was achieved it was only at a heavy cost.

The cost to the people of the Netherlands was huge. Many had been wounded or killed in the battle; much of the town centre area around the bridge at Arnhem and most of Oosterbeek had been flattened – indeed, unexploded grenades, mortars bombs and shells still turn up frequently today. The Germans evacuated the area once the battle was concluded and many more people died of malnutrition and exposure in the hard winter of 1944–5.

It is difficult to find any lessons of real value that were learnt by the British Army. Doubtless a number of practical adjustments were made that had some relevance to the activities of British 6th Airborne and the US XVII Airborne for Operation Plunder, which broke out across the Rhine in March 1945. The stand of 1st Airborne Division at Oosterbeek was a remarkable feat of arms and it made the Parachute Regiment – though, sadly, not the Airlanding Brigade – famous. However, the British Army has been paying a price for this ever since.

A devastated street in Arnhem.

Arnhem in ruins after the battle.

Dutch civilians.

The town centre of Arnhem after the battle.

A parachute landing is only really a device to get infantry onto the battlefield by air, preferably within reach of their objective. Once on the ground, airborne troops have no function that distinguishes them from any other light infantry unit. Throughout the Second World War, British, US and German airborne troops had the misfortune to be deployed to situations that were less than ideal, or for which they were not suited, and suffered accordingly. But their fame – assiduously promoted – has resulted in the preservation of a technique that is long past its sell-by date. The British Parachute Regiment has been of questionable value since 1945. It has consistently demonstrated conspicuous heroism when the opportunity arose – such as that shown by Colonel 'H' Jones in the Falklands – but it is not clear that the regiment has performed better overall than other units with less lustrous reputations. Like any other regiment, it has had its less successful moments. The 1972 Bloody Sunday incident in Northern Ireland owed much to the Parachute Regiment's desire to show other units 'how things should be done', despite a lack of expertise and knowledge of the local situation.

The current structure that includes the Parachute Regiment really exists to protect its role from close scrutiny by politicians anxious to save money, but it has been a very long time since the RAF had the capacity to drop a brigade of paratroops, even without their ancillary units. The application of terms such as 'air-portable' or 'air-mobile' is misleading. The present fleet of helicopters attached to the British armed services is not adequate for delivering anything like three battalions and their specialist supporting arms, so the value of having a parachute brigade at all is questionable at best. At worst, it is a product of bravado and delusions of grandeur about Britain being a world power and 'punching above our weight'.

Ever since 1945, the Parachute Regiment has provided a number of senior British officers – a number out of all proportion to the size of the Parachute Regiment. Often they have been promoted on the recommendation of their predecessors, who have themselves come from the Parachute Regiment, or committees that include a number of Parachute Regiment officers. The result is that many of our most senior army officers have been in a position to protect the regiment from outsiders. The airborne element is still something of a closed shop and resents input of any kind from elsewhere, which is precisely the attitude that prevented proper scrutiny of the quality of training in the units and formations of 1st Airborne Division in 1944.

Whenever defence cuts are in the air – and they so often are – governments are inclined to axe infantry battalions in favour of shiny toys, whose value may be debatable, such as the Trident programme and two new aircraft carriers – with no aircraft. There is never any thought that the Parachute Regiment should be disbanded. The place of the regiment in the public mind, and in the understanding of defence ministers, is, in part, secured by the masterly public relations of the regiment since 1945. And that would not have been possible without the drama of the defeat at Arnhem. The battles around Oosterbeek, and at what is now called

'The John Frost Bridge' (a fitting tribute if ever there was one), exacted a heavy toll at the time and afterwards, but nothing can diminish the actions of the men who fought there with such valour and determination in September 1944.

BIBLIOGRAPHY

Any student of the battle will be aware that this list of works is only the tip of a very large iceberg, and that there are hundred of books that, in part or in whole, describe the battle. These are no more than the ones that have made the most impression on me; it is a wholly subjective selection. I have found each and every one of them to be of great value in forming my view of the events that occurred in and around Arnhem, Oosterbeek, Wolfheze, Renkum and Heelsum in the middle of September 1944.

Bauer, C. *The Battle of Arnhem* (Fonthill, 2013)
Bradley, O. *A Soldier's Story* (Holt, 1951)
Brammall, R. *The Tenth* (Eastgate Publications, 1965)
Brereton, L.H. *The Brereton Diaries* (New York)
Buckingham, W. *Arnhem 1944* (Tempus, 2004)
Chatterton, G. *The Wings of Pegasus* (SFBC, 1990)
Cherry, N. *Arnhem Surgeon* (Brendon Publishing, 2010)
Clark, L. *Arnhem* (Sutton Publishing, 2002)
Deane-Drummond, A. *Return Ticket* (Collins, 1969)
Deeley, G. *Worst Fears Confirmed* (Barny Books, 2005)

Dover, V. *The Silken Canopy* (Cassell, 1979)

Eastwood, S. & Gray, C. & Green, A. *When Dragons Flew* (Silver Link Publishing Ltd., 1994)

Eisenhower, D. *Crusade in Europe* (Knopf-Doubleday, 2013)

Fairley, R. *Remember Arnhem* (Peaton Press)

Faulkner-Brown, H. *A Sapper at Arnhem* (R.N. Sigmond, 2006)

Frost, J. *A Drop Too Many* (Pen & Sword, 2002)

Gibson, R. *Nine Days* (Upfront Publishing Ltd., 2012)

Golden, L. *Echoes From Arnhem* (Kimber, 1984)

Hackett, J. *I Was a Stranger* (Chetto & Windus, 1977)

Hagen, L. *Arnhem Lift* (Hammond, 1955)

Harclerode, P. *Arnhem: A Tragedy of Errors* (Caxton Editions, 2000)

Heaps, L. *The Grey Goose of Arnhem* (Paperjacks, 1977)

Henderson, Dr. D *The Lion and the Eagle* (Cualann, 2001)

Horrocks, B. *A Full Life* (Cooper, 1974)

HMSO *By Air to Battle* (Aztex, 1978)

Jackson, R. *Arnhem: The Battle Remembered* (Airlife Publishing, 1994)

Kent, R. *First In!* (B.T. Batsford, 1979)

Kershaw, R. *It Never Snows in September* (Ian Allan Publishing, 2008)

Lamarque, G. *The Cauldron, 'Zeno'* (Stein & Day, 1966)

Lipmann Kessel, A. *Surgeon At Arms* (Pen & Sword, 2012)

Mawson, S. *Arnhem Doctor* (Spellmount, 2007)

Middlebrook, M. *Arnhem 1944* (Stackpoole Books, 2011)

Montgomery, B. *The Memoirs of Field Marshal Montgomery* (De Capo Press, 1982)

Moynihan, M. *War Correspondent* (Cooper, 1994)

O'Reilly, J.P. *156th Battalion; from Delhi to Arnhem* (2009)

O'Reilly, J.P. *From Delhi to Arnhem* (Thornton, 2009)

Peatling, R. *No Surrender at Arnhem* (Robert Peatling, 2004)

Pielalkiewicz, J. *Arnhem 1944* (1987)

Pijpers, G. & Truesdale, D. *Arnhem: Their Final Battle* (R.N. Sigmond, 2012) Ryan, C. *A Bridge Too Far* (Simon & Schuster, 2010)

Powell, G. *The Devil's Birthday* (Pen & Sword, 2012)

Reinders, P. *No. 1 Forward Observer Unit* (Reinders, 2011)

Reinders, P. *The Polsten Gun at Arnhem* (Reinders, 2005)

Roberts, H. *Capture at Arnhem* (Windrush, 1999)

Roberts, J. *With Spanners Descending* (The Bluecoat Press, 1966)

Sim, J. *Arnhem Spearhead,* (Random House, 1989)

Swiecicki, M. *With the Red Devils at Arnhem* (Helion & Co., 2013)

Turnbull, J. & Hamblett, J. *The Pegasus Patrol* (Tommies Guides, 2009)

Urquhart, R. *Arnhem* (Pen & Sword, 2007)

Urquhart, R. *A Life in Peace and War* (1987)

van Roekel, C. *The Torn Horizon* (J. & W. Ter Horst & C. Van Roekel, 2000)

van Teeseling, P.A. *Over and Over* (2009)

Waddy, J. *A Tour of the Arnhem Battlefields* (Pen & Sword, 1999)

Warrack, G. *Travel by Dark* (Harvill, 1963)

Wilmot, C. *The Struggle for Europe* (Wordsworth Editions, 1997)

Woolacott, R. *Winged Gunners* (Quote Publishers, 1994)

INDEX